erformance Contracting

James Mecklenburger

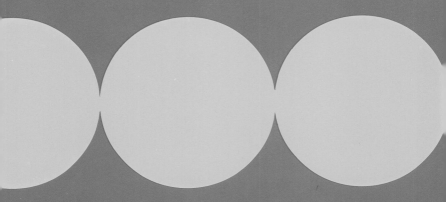

Performance Contracting

THE NATIONAL SOCIETY
FOR THE STUDY OF EDUCATION

Series on Contemporary Educational Issues
Kenneth J. Rehage, Series Editor

The 1971 Titles

Accountability in Education, Leon M. Lessinger and Ralph W. Tyler, Editors
Farewell to Schools??? Daniel U. Levine and Robert J. Havighurst, Editors
Models for Integrated Education, Daniel U. Levine, Editor
PYGMALION Reconsidered, Janet D. Elashoff and Richard E. Snow
Reactions to Silberman's CRISIS IN THE CLASSROOM, A. Harry Passow, Editor

The 1972 Titles

Black Students in White Schools, Edgar A. Epps, Editor
Flexibility in School Programs, Willard J. Congreve and George J. Rinehart, Editors
Performance Contracting—1969-1971, James A. Mecklenburger
The Potential of Educational Futures, Michael Marien and Warren L. Ziegler, Editors
Sex Differences and Discrimination in Education, Scarvia Anderson, Editor

The National Society for the Study of Education also publishes Yearbooks which are distributed by the University of Chicago Press.

Inquiries regarding membership in the Society may be addressed to Kenneth J. Rehage, Secretary-Treasurer, 5835 Kimbark Avenue, Chicago 60637.

Performance Contracting

James A. Mecklenburger
Research Fellow, Indiana University

Charles A. Jones Publishing Company
Worthington, Ohio

2   3   4   5   6   7   8   9   10   /   76   75   74   73

Library of Congress Catalog Card Number: 72-83998
International Standard Book Number: 0-8396-0026-7

Printed in the United States of America

Series Foreword

Performance Contracting—1969-1971 is one of a group of five publications constituting the second set in a series prepared under the auspices of the National Society for the Study of Education. Other titles in this second set of paperbacks dealing with "Contemporary Educational Issues" are:

Sex Differences and Discrimination in Education, edited by Scarvia B. Anderson

Flexibility in School Programs, edited by Willard J. Congreve and George J. Rinehart

Black Students in White Schools, edited by Edgar G. Epps

The Potential of Educational Futures, edited by Michael Marien and Warren L. Ziegler

The response to the first set of five paperbacks in this series, published in 1971, has been very encouraging. Like their predecessors the current volumes, all dealing with timely and significant issues in education, present a useful background and analysis for those who seek a deeper understanding of some of the critical educational problems of our times.

James Mecklenburger has studied the phenomenon of performance contracting intensively. In this book he reports his in-depth study of the first two years of the widely publicized project at the Banneker Elementary school in Gary, Indiana. He draws heavily upon his analysis of relevant documents, extended interviews with persons involved, and his own observations, putting it all together in a thoroughly readable account. He also provides briefer treatments of performance contracts at several other sites, including the well-known Texarkana project.

The Society is grateful to Mr. Mecklenburger for making the results of his interesting study available for inclusion in the series on Contemporary Educational Issues.

Kenneth J. Rehage
for the Committee on the Expanded Publication
Program of the National Society for the Study of Education

Preface

This book explores performance contracting, a small, complex, controversial recent phenomenon in public education. Compared to the billions of dollars invested annually in public schooling, performance contracting has been a miniscule occurrence: a few dozen contracts which all together amount to less than fifteen million dollars. Yet performance contracting has had cast upon it attention, emotion, and criticism far in excess of what its size might lead one to expect. Various organizations have spoken vehemently, branding performance contracting as hucksterism, a hoax, or part of a plot to destroy public education.

In a typical performance contract, a school system subcontracts a portion of its instructional task—usually the teaching of reading to disadvantaged youngsters—and agrees to pay the contractor according to the contractor's success at causing children to learn. Contractors usually have been private "learning companies" but some have been teachers, teachers associations, or administrators.

In one sense, performance contracting is a *practice,* just as modular scheduling or transporting children by school bus is a practice. It is often depicted as a series of tasks, procedures, and processes with esoteric names—RFP (request for proposals), bidders conference, needs assessment, educational accomplishment audit, and turnkey, to name a few. In another sense, performance contracting is a *political-historical event,* just as is school bussing to achieve integration of the races. One could say that performance contracting is what occurred in Texarkana in 1969, in Gary in 1970, and elsewhere under sponsorship of the Office of Economic Opportunity during 1970-1971.

As a *concept,* performance contracting derives from such conceptual schemes as scientific management, instructional technology, general systems theory, and behavioral psychology. It appeals to advocates of each of these, and has inherited a potpourri of terminology from them. Also performance contracting has reflected moral or philosophical ideas about childhood, motivation, learning, curriculum, and the social purpose of schools which appeal to advocates of these conceptual schemes.

The first performance contract occurred in Texarkana and received nationwide publicity during 1969-1970, so that for a time, the term "Texarkana" became synonymous with the new phenomenon of "performance contracting." Other important contracts occurred during 1970-1971 in Virginia, Colorado, Michigan, Florida, Texas, Massachusetts, Maine, Rhode Island, and California, and each merits a share of attention later in this book. This narrative, however, slights chronology in favor of beginning with the most revealing example of performance contracting. The epitome of performance contracting occurred in the Banneker Elementary school—now the Banneker Contracted Curriculum Center—in Gary, Indiana. In 1971, "Banneker" replaced "Texarkana" in the public eye as synonymous with performance contracting. More important, virtually the entire realm of the performance contract experience—the practices, the politics, the strengths, the flaws, and the controversies—is visible in the history of the Banneker project.

What began in the fall of 1970 as a one-time student project to describe the performance contract in Gary has become for me a journalistic mini-career. In this book I report what I have learned as impartially as I can.

James A. Mecklenburger

Contents

Part Three: Texarkana

Part One

Introduction

Origins
of Performance
Contracting

Performance contracting did not spring into the world unsired. It had several ancestors, both near and distant.

Educational Technology

Pedagogically, spiritually, and linguistically, performance contracts have borrowed heavily from the ideas and practices of the "educational technology" enterprise: programmed instruction, individualized instruction, differentiated staffing. behavioral objectives, teaching machines, instructional systems, computer-managed instruction, team teaching, behavioral modification, and the like. Each and all of these ideas and practices manifest the same results-oriented, problem-solving, pragmatic perspective which is variously called technology, management, engineering, good old American know-how, the systems approach, and other names.

During the 1960's, many corporations and a number of voices within the educational establishment (such as the Regional Educational Laboratories) urged that technological attitudes be adopted in education. Generally, the response was cool and cautious. However, during the 1960's educational technology fared far better within military and industrial settings, and in Job Corps and remedial programs. Most of the private corporations who entered or bid for performance contracts during 1969 to 1971 had shared earlier experience in military, industrial, Job Corps, and other nonpublic school arenas in which they had entered contracts to provide instructional services.

Similarly, many of the school superintendents who adopted performance contracting are sympathetic to patterns of school operation modelled after other large enterprises. Not surprisingly, advocates of performance contracts and hostile critics alike have perceived the kinship of performance contracting with the Apollo program, Defense Department procurement practices, IBM, General Motors, Rand Corporation, and other symbols of "modern technological society."

Emanuel Kafka of the New York Teachers Association, for example, castigated technological intrusions into schools:

> Westinghouse, Borg-Warner, and all the rest of the military-industrial complex are not moving on the public schools because they have developed an aching social concern. They are closing on the minds of children now for the same reason they have before produced napalm and Thalidomide, and polluted our rivers, our air, and our entire environment. They are driven by an insatiable hunger for constantly bigger profits. (1)

And Leon Lessinger, former associate commissioner of education in the U. S. Office of Education, praised a technological approach to education:

> Since World War II several fields have been developed to enable leaders of very complex enterprises to operate effectively and efficiently. These emerging fields include: systems design and analysis, management by objectives, contract engineering (including warrantees, performance contracts and incentives), logistics, quality assurance, value engineering, and the like. The coordination of these fields around educational concerns for an improved technology of instruction may be conveniently called educational engineering. . . . Engineering has traditionally been a problem-solving activity, a profession dedicated to harnessing and creating technology to the accomplishment of desired ends. . . . The heart of the educational engineering process is the performance contract. (2)

This management/business/technological flavor to performance contracting, coupled with taxpayer revolt and budget crises in public schools, has served to highlight economic components of performance contracting. Many projects emphasized cost-effectiveness. The Texarkana school boards chose among competing proposals by selecting the cheapest. The Gary school board insisted that Banneker "costs no more." President Nixon and administration spokesmen have urged increased accountability rather than increased appropriations. Two Rand Corporation economists explained the concept of performance contracting in economic terms of "risk," "cost," and "incentives." (3) Charles Blaschke, who introduced the performance contract idea to Texarkana school officials, said the Defense Department learned long ago "that performance contracting through competitive bidding was the closest approximation to the market mechanism, ensuring disinterested procurement of efficient goods and services." (4) Critics also see economic implications and point to the Defense Department cost overruns and the C5A transport.

Publisher's Weekly editorialized,

In the consumer goods field, there is a tradition, not always observed, that if a newly purchased product does not perform as promised, it may be returned for repair, replacement or refund. The consumer has a reasonable guarantee, in short, of his money's worth. The "money's worth" line of thinking has now entered the field of American education. (5)

In this context, the most well known performance contract has been offered for several years by Evelyn Wood Reading Dynamics: triple your reading rate, or your money back.

Historical Parallels

"There is by now," said the editor of *Urban Education,* "some decently documented history which says that schoolmen emulate businessmen when businessmen enjoy esteem." (6) From this viewpoint, educational technology generally, and performance contracting specifically, are sometimes characterized or dismissed as latter-day versions of "scientific management." No doubt, there are obvious parallels.

For example, Herbert M. Kliebard describes the 1910's and 1920's as a time of "growing acceptance of a powerful and restrictive bureaucratic model for education which looked toward the management techniques of industry as its ideal of excellence and source of inspiration." (7)

Kliebard notes that efficiency, business techniques, and effectiveness of instruction were the cornerstones of John Franklin Bobbitt's influential curriculum theory. Bobbitt's principle, "educate the individual according to his capabilities", (8) rings close to today's individualized instruction, which urges that each child proceed at his own rate. Bobbitt, in 1912, like Lessinger today, spoke of needed "educational engineers." (9) In 1920, Bobbitt wrote,

In the world of economic production, a major secret of success is predetermination. . . . The business world is institutionalizing foresight. . . . There is a growing realization within the educational profession that we must particularize the objectives of education. We too must institutionalize foresight. (10)

Kliebard observes that while Bobbitt's influence waned in the 1930's, his intellectual heirs have revived in the 1960's advocating technology, systems approaches, and the like.

The drift of Kliebard's argument is anti-technological. "The bureaucratic model," he says, "along with its behavioristic and technological refinements, threatens to destroy in the name of efficiency, the satisfaction that one may find in intellectual activity."

The mechanistic conception of man, the technology-systems analysis approach to human affairs, the production metaphor for curriculum design all share a common perspective. They represent a deterministic outlook on human behavior. . . . As Von Bertalanffy put it, "Stimulus-response, input-output, producer-consumer are all the same concepts, only expressed in different terms . . . people are manipulated as they deserve, that is, as overgrown Skinner rats." (11)

Kliebard and many other critics who have posed a dichotomy between technology and humanism, have chosen the latter position and assume, therefore, that technological approaches must be regarded negatively. These arguments have been advanced against performance contracting frequently, especially by spokesmen for the American Federation of Teachers.

But even if one discounts Kliebard's conclusions about technology, the parallels he sees between earlier events and contemporary ones are striking. It is worth noting too that much of the impetus for what is called educational technology comes from B. F. Skinner and his colleagues; many of those involved in performance contracting identify themselves or their instructional techniques as Skinnerian. (12)

Some have searched for the lessons of history beyond American shores and before the twentieth century. They see parallels in nineteenth century attempts at payment by results. Gladys Harding finds payment by results was tried and abandoned in England. (13) Charles Phillips reports the same history in Canada. (14) Others think they find a parallel in recent Russian experiments. (15) In every case, severe criticism eventually arose because the use of payment by test results narrowed teaching to the content of the test and encouraged other kinds of chicanery. Thus the "teaching to the test" accusations levelled at performance contracts in Texarkana and Providence have some precedent. Others, closer to home, have seen a parallel in the New York State Regents Examination.

Whatever its ancestry, performance contracting has taken on a life of its own within public education. Still, its roots in technological ideas, practices and personnel are apparent. One sees them in the procedures for entering a performance contract, in the rhetoric of school board members and federal officials who advocate performance contracts, in the pedagogical techniques selected by contractors, and in the basic principle of performance contracting—linking money spent to measurable educational results. Similarly, most opposition to performance contracting has advanced anti-technological arguments.

Notes

(1) E. Kafka, press release, New York State Teachers Association, November 13, 1970. Contains testimony before the New York State Commission on the Quality, Cost and Financing of Elementary and Secondary Education. Mr. Kafka is president of the New York State Teachers Association.

(2) L. Lessinger, "Focus on the Learner: Central Concern of Accountability in Education," *Audiovisual Instruction,* 15 (June-July 1970): 43-44.

(3) J. P. Stucker, and G. R. Hall, *The Performance Contracting Concept in Education* (Santa Monica: Rand Corporation, 1971), pp. 5-12.

(4) C. Blaschke, "Competitive Bidding and Turnkey Operations," *Education Turnkey News*, 1 (April 1970): 1.

(5) R. H. Smith, "In Education are Publishers Accountable?", *Publisher's Weekly*, 199 (January 18, 1971): 113. Reprinted by permission of R. R. Bowker Company, a Xerox Company, copyright © 1971 by Xerox Corporation.

(6) W. Button, "Performance Contracting: Some Reservations," *Urban Education*, 5, No. 4 (January 1971): 307-308. Reprinted by permission of the publisher, Sage Publications, Inc.

(7) H. M. Kliebard, "Bureaucracy and Curriculum Theory," *Freedom, Bureaucracy, and Schooling*, 1971 Yearbook of the Association for Supervision and Curriculum Development, Washington, D. C., 1971, p. 74.

(8) J. F. Bobbitt, "The Elimination of Waste in Education," *The Elementary School Teacher*, 12 (February 1912): 260.

(9) Ibid., p. 264.

(10) J. F. Bobbitt, "The Objectives of Secondary Education," *The School Review*, 12 (December 1920): 738.

(11) Kliebard, "Bureaucracy and Curriculum Theory," p. 93, Citing L. V. Bertalanffy, *Robots, Men and Minds: Psychology in the Modern World* (New York: G. Braziller, 1967), p. 12.

(12) See, for example, B. F. Frieder, "Motivation and Performance Contracting," *Journal of Research and Development in Education*, 5 (Fall 1971): 49-61.

(13) G. Harding, "A Hundred Years Before Texarkana," *The Journal of Educational Research*, 64 (May-June 1971): cover.

(14) C. E. Phillips, *The Development of Education in Canada* (Toronto: W. J. Gage and Company Limited, 1957), pp. 512-14.

(15) "Schools Sign Private Firms to Help Poor Pupils Learn," *The Baltimore Sun*, March 1, 1971, p. 1.

Part Two

Banneker

II

Overview

Performance Contracts as Drama

Phileas Fogg circumnavigated the globe in a race to break the astounding mark of eighty days, in Jules Verne's *Around the World in Eighty Days.* Conventional wisdom said it was impossible. The wager staked Fogg's canny intelligence against the imperfect technology of travel; money hung in the balance.

In that elemental conflict lay drama. So too with performance contracts such as those in Texarkana and Gary, Indiana.

Behavioral Research Laboratories (BRL), a private corporation, has taken charge of Gary's Banneker Elementary School to cause poor learners to learn more in less time. The wager stakes the inventiveness of BRL against the imperfect technology of teaching. More than two million dollars hangs in the balance. The drama is apparent: "Results or Else," a newspaper headline phrased it. (1) Banneker School was chosen for the four-year multi-million dollar performance contract between Gary schools and BRL. (For the sake of brevity, and consistent with popular usage, this book will employ the term "Banneker" to designate the project.)

In the fall of 1971, bankruptcy and closing of the Gary Public Schools seemed imminent. A BRL official indicated that Banneker would *not* close and that, if necessary, BRL would pay the cost of keeping that school open. This unique arrangement never had to be made, for the State of Indiana bailed out the school district.

Banneker, like Texarkana before it, is a grandstand play, a larger-than-life drama. Its implications gather powerful friends and create powerful enemies—each with his own just cause and his own theatrical flair. Mrs. Coretta Scott King awarded the first annual Achievement Award, sponsored by the Martin Luther King Jr. Memorial Center, to Banneker School "for its commitment in expanding educational opportunities for inner city children." (2) The Gary Teachers Union threatened to strike as it claimed, rightly, that the Banneker program infringed its agreement with the Gary board of education. The State of Indiana, for one month during 1971, dropped Banneker School from the Indiana public school system.

Performance Contracts as Politics

"I didn't know *how* political education could be," a graduate student at Northwestern studying Banneker remarked, "until I started researching this topic."

"Education is in politics up to its neck," says Nolan Estes, superintendent of schools in Dallas (where there have been several performance contracts) who is also a former associate commissioner of education in the U. S. Office of Education. He added

The name of the game is *conflict*, and those who cannot accept the prospect of entering into public debate to argue for the programs which they are convinced will improve education, and to submit fact, rational analysis, and empirical evidence to buttress their convictions, would do well to leave the public education arena before they get hurt. (3)

Few educators are more adept in the politics of conflict than some who created Banneker and some who opposed it. Banneker has a history of conflict, some veiled from public view and some fought in newspaper headlines. In the exigencies of politics, plain sense suggested muting certain facts; however, because such pragmatic wisdom runs counter to idealistic conventions about openness and truth, the parties involved in Banneker have found it easy to accuse each other of misrepresentation, distortion and engaging in "politics."

Despite talk of public accountability, the superintendent, the Gary Teachers Union, and Behavioral Research Laboratories each played the cards close to the vest over Banneker. This is a characteristic Gary manner of "doing business for kids" (4) for Gary sees itself as "a community of 180,000 people that has to fight the world sometimes to get certain things done for children." (5) Peter Schrag, commenting on the public's "Right to Know," asserted that secretiveness, obfuscation, and news management are typical of big city schools. (6) One Gary administrator, remarking on my *Phi Delta Kappan* (7) report on Banneker, told me, "I was aghast at the fact that you hit so many nails right on the head," for particularly in the early—and troubled—months of the Banneker project, it was difficult for visitors to peer beyond the "party line" and see Banneker as those involved saw it.

Performance Contracts
as Cocktail Party Conversation

Coincident with the publicity surrounding the projects, the names "Banneker" and "Texarkana" were invoked by friends and enemies, in a hundred written or conversational contexts, to prove most any point. Often, they simply popped up in a passing phrase: "revolutionary change, such as Banneker" or "business taking over schools, like Texarkana." What actually occurred in these projects was frequently less important to people than what was said about them. Therefore many of the anecdotes, opinions, allusions, praises, claims, criticisms, and analyses one hears or reads are grounded in presumption, ignorance, and misunderstanding. To pursue the drama analogy, talk about performance contracts often resembled talk about *Hair* or *Jesus Christ, Superstar,* as the titles took on life quite divorced from the plays—or contracts—themselves.

Because of this gap between fact and discussion, the public perception of performance contracts does not always resemble what occurred.

Notes

(1) "Brand New Approach to School Problems: Guaranteed Learning—Results or Else," *Louisville Courier-Journal,* February 3, 1970.

(2) "School in Indiana Wins King Award," *The Atlanta Journal,* July 1, 1971.

(3) N. Estes, "The New Rules of Boardmanship," *American School Board Journal,* 157 (February 1970): 17-18.

(4) The phrase is Edward Pino's, superintendent of schools in Cherry Creek, Colorado, in "Individual Performance-Based Teachers Contracts," a speech at the Accountability and Performance Contracting in Reading Conference, Indiana University, March 22, 1971.

(5) Stated by Otha Porter, assistant superintendent in Gary, in an interview with the author, at Gary, Indiana, December, 1970.

(6) P. Schrag, "The Right to Know," *Saturday Review,* 54 (December 18, 1971): 53. ©1971 Saturday Review, Inc.

(7) J. A. Mecklenburger and J. A. Wilson, "The Performance Contract in Gary," *Phi Delta Kappan,* 52 (March 1971): 406-410.

III

The Genesis of Banneker

Gordon McAndrew

Rand Corporation, under a $300,000 grant from the Department of Health, Education and Welfare, studied performance contracting during 1970-1971. (1) In each of the cities Rand studied, "A respected and influential 'sponsor' within the school district" played a vital role in championing the performance contract there. (2)

That "sponsor," in Gary, was Gordon McAndrew, superintendent of schools. He helped conceive the Banneker performance contract, he sold it to the school board, he advised the press, and he acted as troubleshooter. This performance contract with Behavioral Research Laboratories was his project; Banneker obviously reflected his style and became associated with him in the public mind.

The Office of Economic Opportunity announced its nationwide performance contract experiment in July, 1970. When McAndrew announced Banneker the next week, Banneker seemed more daring, more controversial, and more spectacular. Banneker was reported in *Newsweek* (and elsewhere) as McAndrew's triumphant gambit:

When Gordon McAndrew took over as superintendent of schools in Gary, Indiana, two years ago, he discovered that three out of four children in the inner city could not read at normal grade level. "I kept thinking about the U. S. Steel plant here," he recalls. "If 75 percent of their ingots came out defective, they would change." So McAndrew, backed by a school board willing to gamble, made a daring change: beginning this fall, the total operation of one of Gary's elementary schools will be placed in the hands of a private company to see if someone else can teach the kids how to read, write and cipher the way they should. (3)

The industrial metaphor in McAndrew's remarks (not just in *Newsweek*) with its implied comparison of students to ingots, and the hint that children should conform to specifications, is a popular figure of speech in Gary, certainly indicative of an approach to schooling that McAndrew shares with several members of the school board. (4) It is not unique to Banneker; nor is it a particularly apt metaphor. But the mass media linked such statements to Banneker, making it appear singularly mechanistic and dehumanizing.

The American Federation of Teachers and the Gary Teachers Union

Such statements occurred coincidentally with the national convention of the American Federation of Teachers (AFT), an organization not disposed to such metaphors. In addition, the arrival of corporate "outsiders" such as BRL in the schools carried implied accusations of teacher imcompetence, and implied a threat to the union position in collective bargaining.

The style of such rhetoric, as much as its substance, aggravated the AFT—not only rhetoric from Gary but from the Office of Economic Opportunity as well. In convention in August, the AFT resolved:

That the AFT go on record as opposing any plan, such as performance contracting, which

1) will take the determination of education policy out of the hands of the public and place it in the hands of private industrial entrepreneurs,
2) threatens to establish a monopoly of education by big business,
3) threatens to dehumanize the learning process,
4) would sow distrust among teachers through a structured incentive program,
5) promotes "teaching to the (standardized) test,"
6) subverts the collective bargaining process and reduces teacher input, and
7) is predicated on the assumption that education achievement can be improved in the vacuum of a machine-oriented classroom, without changing the wider environment of the poverty-stricken child. (5)

The union journal, *The American Teacher,* headlined "Hucksters in the Schools" in September, "Education Under Siege" in October, "Judgement Day in the Schools" in November, and so on.

Gary teachers are almost 100 percent AFT members. The union is tough, and after many skirmishes and a four-week strike in the spring of 1970, the union did not regard McAndrew as its friend. Union officials spoke of a "credibility gap." McAndrew, in turn, described the relationship between the union and the schools as a "counterproductive adversary relationship." (6)

Charles O. Smith was president of the Gary Teachers Union and also an AFT vice-president. The AFT announced in November a system to monitor the further extension of private enterprise into the public schools. Smith became the monitoring post for the central United States.

In fact, there proved to be little influx of new information to the central U. S. monitoring post; but Smith indicated he spent 20 percent of his time just talking to people about Banneker. (7)

Particularly during the first semester, Smith was an excellent source of first-hand information about Banneker; he had free access while most visitors did not get beyond the front office except on a closely guided tour.

McAndrew, recounting the history of Banneker, said,

I talked with the teachers union before the proposal ever went to the board. My feeling was that they were not particularly hot about the idea. What I wanted them to do was join with us, because I knew there would be questions of contract involved in this. For their own reasons, they did not really feel they should go along. Now, I think, they accuse me of ramming it down their throats. Be that as it may, we started in the fall. (8)

The State Superintendency

McAndrew anticipated conflict with the union as well as with the Indiana State Department of Public Instruction. In general, Gary does not fare well at the state capitol. Indiana is a rural, conservative state in which whites and Republicans dominate. Militant, impatient, impoverished Gary, in the state's northwest corner, black and Democratic, receives little sympathetic hearing. In addition, Richard D. Wells, the State Superintendent of Public Instruction, made no secret of his disapproval of Banneker.

Much that has been written elsewhere about the conflict between Gary and the State of Indiana over Banneker takes that confrontation at face value. But as much as issues were involved, the confrontation was a sparring match also, for which Banneker was more the excuse than the cause. Wells was defeated in a reelection bid in November, 1970, but served until March 15. When Wells left office in 1971, the Banneker conflict subsided and by autumn of 1971, the State Department and Gary were working closely together. Banneker was regarded more sympathetically by the new state superintendent, John Loughlin.

BRL and its President, George Stern

Behavioral Research Laboratories is a company developed in the early 1960's by entrepreneurs with a mission. *Look* described M. W. Sullivan, founder of BRL, and his associates as out "to kill Dick and Jane . . . to kill the mind-squashing assumptions and practices that have retarded American education from the beginning." (9) George Stern, who became president of BRL in 1969 after five years with the company, thrives on conflict and, like McAndrew, usually wins. They are kindred spirits.

While they underestimated the intensity of the conflict, McAndrew and Stern began Banneker with the presumption that attacks by the union and the State of Indiana were inevitable. Each has said that in his estimation had they not plunged into the project quickly, the State and the union would have killed it.

But why enter this battleground at all? The apparent answer, that BRL stood to make a substantial profit on site in Gary, will not suffice. Even had BRL not run into additional expense, BRL could do little more than break even on its Banneker contract. BRL could expect other sales, of course, if Banneker proved successful, which may have justified the risk. It was a mild risk since Banneker amounted to perhaps 5 percent of BRL business. (10) But Banneker consumed Stern's attention more than 5 percent; within the company, Banneker was his baby. For a company with a mission, Banneker was an irresistible opportunity; as George Stern said, "This contract gives us the clout to implement all our ideas." (11)

McAndrew narrated the genesis of Banneker this way:

Actually, BRL was here before I got here (in 1968). They were doing some summer programs with seventh grade kids, underachievers.

When I was looking around at the data on the results of various programs, the one program that seemed to show some glimmer was that one, the summer reading program using Sullivan materials. As a result of that, I thought we ought to try a little more extensively, and therefore last fall we put the Sullivan reading materials into half a dozen elementary schools. And the evidence we have on this is pretty good.

Well, during the course of talking to BRL people about that, I got to know the president of the company, a guy named George Stern. George and I got to talking once, and somehow or other we got to chatting about what we thought about this whole "accountability" notion. He had indicated they were kind of getting into some of that.

Out of that conversation came the idea of a school, an existing school, and I said (I said it kind of facetiously at the beginning), "Tell you what. We'll contract with you to do this on a schoolwide basis—not just reading but the whole shebang, with two conditions: one, it can't cost any more money than we're now spending and two, that you have to take a school as it now exists."

Out of that came a proposal. From that point on it was a matter of negotiating and getting the details worked out.

That was when I recommended it and the board said, "Go, and work out this kind of thing." They left up to me the details, the timing, the how you do it. At that point we hadn't even had the school chosen. It was just an idea they were approving in principle. (12)

Why hadn't the program been opened to competitive bidding as the Texarkana project had been and as several advocates of performance contracts suggest?

I did talk with a couple of other firms. And they indicated that they would not be interested. They said they didn't want to do it on that school basis, which was the only way I wanted to do it.

I think the other thing was that I knew something about the BRL program. I think also, in talking with Stern and some of his people, I felt they kind of "grabbed" the concept as well as I did. (13)

George Stern told me substantially the same story, but others saw it differently. While the merchandising methods of BRL were clearly very successful, both the methods used by BRL and methods employed to select BRL as the contractor were regarded by some critics as totally indefensible.

Gary's Racial Tone

Nothing in the Gary schools, especially the school board's interest in Banneker, can be appreciated separately from the racial tone there. In the late 1960's, the black minority in Gary became the majority and elected a black mayor, Richard Hatcher, who enjoys local and national prominence. In Gary, the mayor appoints the school board, which after Hatcher's election gained a black majority and a strong-willed black president. (Illustrative of the tensions in Gary, state senator Bernard Konrady, who represents the white minority in Gary and who had criticized McAndrew and the school board for ruining the schools, entered a motion in the state legislature to revise the method of appointing school board members. He lost.)

The one white member of the board, at the time of Banneker's approval, was Theodore Nering. When his term expired some months later, he was not reappointed by Hatcher, which was to be expected, inasmuch as he hadn't had a motion seconded at a board meeting since the black majority took over. He became the Republican candidate for mayor and lost handily to Hatcher.

Nering recounted the board approval of Banneker this way:

I never voted against it, but I didn't vote for it. And the reasons that I didn't vote for it were, for example, we didn't have any competition on this; we didn't have a chance to look at somebody else's program. I brought this up in a public meeting and Gordon McAndrew thought that this group was most satisfactory, and from his observation and understanding, there wasn't the need or the necessity to talk to someone else. I still thought we should have.

Secondly, I thought I—and even the rest of the board—did not really understand this program. I felt that the board didn't know enough about it, and I also felt the administration didn't know enough about it.

They wanted to get the program started in the fall, to get the show on the road. But we weren't in the position of being sure of ourselves at the time we made our decision. But since this deadline had to be met—at least *they* felt it had to be met—the decision was made. (14)

"There's probably not a board of education in Indiana more stubborn than Gary's once it's made up its mind to do something," one Gary administrator confided to me. Alfonso Holliday, the Board's 1970-1971 president, makes this clear, as he described "why the Gary school board bought it":

When you're at the bottom, all you can do is look up and try something different. We must be willing to be pioneers and no longer say our children can't learn.

You can't in good conscience be a rubber stamp for continuing educational practices that are not working. . . . I think the public likes the fact that as a board we make decisions on key issues. We don't "committee" problems and study them to death. We want the public to know where we stand—because people, not teacher groups, should control the schools.

School boards must stand their ground for what is best for kids in their system, no matter who is doing the complaining. Too many boards tend to be intimidated by teacher unions or associations. (15)

Right to Learn, "Accountability" and Texarkana

If drama and performance contracts alike are shaped by the actors who give them life and by their audience, as we have seen in the case of Banneker, they also are shaped by chance occurrences, prevailing attitudes, and new ideas.

"All young people in our schools, regardless of color or condition, can and will learn and our job is to teach them." Gordon McAndrew submitted this policy proposal, entitled RIGHT TO LEARN, on March 9, 1970, and urged his school board that all educational programs should be "founded on this commitment."

President Nixon had urged the same commitment a week earlier, in his March 3rd educational reform message to Congress:

Apart from the general public interest in providing teachers an honorable and well paid professional career, there is only one important question to be added about education: What do the children learn? . . .

From these considerations we derive another new concept: *accountability.* School administrators and school teachers alike are responsible for their performance, and it is in their interest as well as in the interests of their pupils that they be held accountable.

Early results from the first performance contract, in Texarkana, had reaped national headlines in February. This publicity reinforced the rhetoric surrounding Texarkana that private corporations could be held accountable in a way that schools had not been: no results, no money.

The conversations McAndrew described (see p. 14) between himself and George Stern that resulted in the agreement to performance contract an entire school occurred within this short space of time—between the Texarkana results, the Nixon speech, and the RIGHT TO LEARN policy.

The time was ripe for an innovative superintendent such as McAndrew to link money with school success—especially a black school. To some, it appeared in retrospect, as a somewhat giddy moment, in which prudence was eroded by enthusiasm. Claims were made and attitudes fostered which in soberer moments a year later seemed extreme or regrettable. But the basic spirit to which performance contracting appealed—not just in Gary, but in the federal government, in Grand Rapids, in Dallas, in Cherry Creek, and elsewhere—was a "can do" and "good-old-American-know-how" spirit. To this the Gary board of education was responsive, as were others. At that moment and in that mood, the Gary board approved a performance contract project.

The BRL Proposal and Reactions to It

The BRL proposal was submitted to Gary on June first. It emphasized both the RIGHT TO LEARN policy and "accountability." BRL began its proposal with these words from McAndrew's policy statement:

The single most serious educational problem in the Gary schools is widespread and consistent underachievement, particularly in the basic learning skills.

The RIGHT TO LEARN program, therefore, is based on two related and complementary priorities: 1) teaching the fundamentals, with particular emphasis on reading and language development and 2) fostering in students positive attitudes and motivation for learning. (16)

Moreover, BRL claimed

The need to introduce "accountability" into the public schools has long been recognized by educators and laymen. Until the recent development of educational systems companies such as Behavioral Research Laboratories, there have been few ways to give the concept of accountability real meaning in the public schools. (17)

Accordingly, BRL proposed "a subcontracted program that guarantees achievement in the fundamental skills." (18)

Rereading the proposal a year later, or the early press releases about Banneker, or any other performance contract, one still becomes swept up by the optimistic elan, the impatience to get in there and make those kids learn. Like Phileas Fogg heading off on his journey around the world, grim realities were for the moment overlooked. The commitment to *do* the thing at all was heady enough.

The genius stroke, in the early months of the performance contract phenomenon—the logical extension of a "can-do" mentality—was the use of the term "guarantee." Some writers adopted the term "guaranteed performance contracting."

"Guarantee" communicated a sense of self-confidence on the part of learning companies that seemed a breath of fresh air to harried administrators, school boards, and some state and federal bureaucrats. "Guarantee" meant these companies might actually have the expertise to solve the dilemma of underachievement. "Guarantee" meant somebody else beside the school authorities could be blamed in the event of failure. "Guarantee" was reminiscent enough of advertising claims for consumer products that it gave the school authorities confidence in their decision to buy. For example, "When an organization in which one has confidence says 'We think we can do something about achievement, and we'll guarantee the results,' then I think it would be criminal for the school system not to give them an opportunity," Assistant Superintendent Otha Porter said in October. (19)

Performance contractors, including BRL, implied they had a panacea (or at least did not deny it), and school boards who bought performance contracts often abandoned the soft sell. "For the first time, we had a school where either the children learn or we get out money back," said the Gary board president. (20) The former principal of Banneker, who became "learning director," Clarence Benford, told the *New York Times* in July, 1970, "With the company's guarantee, we feel we have everything to gain and nothing to lose." (21)

Teachers were skeptical—for good reasons. They had worked in these schools, knew the problems, had fought the earlier battles for changes in these schools, had even used the instructional materials offered by the contractors. Appropriately, when the Gary board invited the union to take a school under the same arrangements made with the contractor, the union turned the offer down.

Not only did teachers see performance contracts as an affront, a threat, and beneath their dignity; beyond these irritations, teachers were upset by the contractors' claims to being efficient. If BRL, for example, had claimed it would get better results at 50 percent more cost, teacher organizations might have responded more calmly. They, after all, have made that same claim for years: better schools cost more money. The AFT's More Effective Schools program, which McAndrew said the union proposed as an alternative to Banneker, may cost 100 percent more.

Preconditions: Cost and Test Scores

BRL and McAndrew, for demanding political reasons, deferred to prevailing attitude about school cost and insisted that Banneker "costs no more." As McAndrew remembered, this had been one of his preconditions to Stern. McAndrew said in October, 1970, that he was attracted to the program by its accountability and the fact that it costs no more. (22) A year later he was still saying it. (23) No wonder. In Gary, during the first year of the Banneker program, the school district nearly suffered a payday-less Christmas. The second year the district faced bankruptcy with an $11 million deficit. Under these circumstances any new program which cost more than normal would be politically traumatic for the school administration.

While cost was an explicit precondition, guaranteed gains in standardized achievement test scores were also required. People believe in these scores in Gary and educational programs are justified on the basis of them. Racial attitudes reinforce this: most white students score better than most black students, which pleases white prejudices; blacks often expressed the reverse psychology to me, that the schools must make black students succeed on the white man's terms. One school principal in Gary said "The people that put stock in the scores are the superintendent and the school board, because they want all the kids up here—above the norm." (24) In a system-wide memo entitled "Why Banneker?", McAndrew explained the decision by displaying a chart of sixth-grade mean grade-equivalent scores on the Iowa Basic Skills test. He said

In noting that Banneker School was third from the bottom in achievement scores, as indicated in the accompanying chart, the Board at its last meeting recommended that test data be distributed to all teachers so that they might know what the problems are that we are trying to solve. (25)

Similarly, explaining the purpose of the project, McAndrew said, "I wasn't interested in developing all kinds of fancy objectives; what I want to know is, can we teach kids to read and add? And here's a school where 75 percent of them can't. That's the objective." (26)

In light of prevailing attitudes toward cost and testing, it is no wonder that BRL proposed

that striking improvement can be made at no increase in cost. Therefore, the total annual charge per pupil under this contract will be $800, the average amount now spent per inner city pupil in Gary. . . . Assuming a total student population of 800 students, the maximum annual cost of the program (if all students succeed) will be $640,000 an amount equal to what is currently spent on the education of a similar population in Gary.

At the end of three years, BRL will refund the entire fee paid for any child who has participated in the program for three years but has not achieved at or above national norms as determined by standardized instruments. (27)

One irony in this approach, spawned as it was by early reports from Texarkana, is that during the summer before Banneker began, the Texarkana project ended in a scandal over testing, with the cost of that program hanging in the balance.

From then on, every performance contract acquired a cloud of suspicion about testing. To many observers, issues of testing are sufficient to invalidate the entire concept of performance contracting. As the Rand study diplomatically phrased it,

Performance contracting has exacerbated old problems to the point where they almost seem to be new ones. The most severe have been legal questions, issues of teacher status, difficulties in supplying the needed management skills, and *especially, problems of test selection and administration.* (Italics added.) (28)

Two of seven chapters of conclusions and implications in the Rand study dwell on the thorny issue of measuring performance in performance contracts.

The "real" cost of Banneker has been equally suspect as the Gary Teachers Union, the AFT, and for a time the Indiana Department of Public Instruction, all anxious to discredit the project, energetically demonstrated that "costs no more" is a misrepresentation. Which it is.

BRL Introduces
"The Systems Approach"

In discussing accountability, BRL stated that "Until the recent development of educational systems companies such as Behavioral Research Laboratories . . ." there was no way to get accountability. (29) BRL, and most other companies who entered performance contracts, falls within that coterie of school reformers who think systems approaches can be applied to schools, just as they have been in other institutions, especially in large business and the defense industry. Performance contracting has appealed mostly to "educational systems companies" who found, in the circumstances of a performance contract, a means to implement their ideas.

Systems approaches vary; the term does not designate something precise. Systems represents a formalization of common sense, an adaptation of scientific thinking to management of organizations.

Systems connotes goal-oriented thinking, but on any scale from immense efforts such as NASA to small efforts such as managing a classroom. A system strives toward a goal (or goals), organizes itself to reach that goal, and is evaluated in terms of that goal. Evaluation makes a system self-correcting, striving toward more adequately fulfilling its purposes.

Applied to schools, systems approaches will necessarily seek to identify the goal(s) of schooling. Generally, the conclusion is that "learning" is the goal, that "schools exist to produce learning." One hastens to add that this is not the only possible answer, but most concern with instructional systems assumes this answer, as BRL did. BRL called its systems approach PROJECT LEARN in which the "student is placed at the center of the system, and the system modifies its instructional techniques to accommodate his learning strategies." (30)

What BRL brought to Banneker was PROJECT READ and PROJECT MATH plus PROJECT LEARN. The first two are lengthy sequences of programmed instruction (which, itself, is a kind of "system") through which students can move individually at their own rate. Diagnostic tests determine what each student already can do, what he needs to learn, and place him at an appropriate place in the programmed sequence. PROJECT LEARN, however, is not a product; it is a style of operation that really must be re-created wherever it is applied. PROJECT LEARN is not an "off the shelf" product as are PROJECT READ and PROJECT MATH. This fact was not communicated in the BRL proposal; indeed, the opposite is implied.

Even a fairly thorough reading of the proposal leaves one the impression that BRL would arrive at Banneker and immediately institute a radically new kind of school. The BRL proposal states what will be done—community involvement, staff development through preservice and inservice training, individualized instruction, nongraded classrooms, differentiated staffing, and more. The proposal does not say how long this takes; it only says that "The Gary Contracted Curriculum Center offers a method that enables School City to achieve many of the goals of its RIGHT TO LEARN program within a relatively brief time." (31)

Not to say that BRL did not have ideas; it surely did. And BRL had some experience with some of these ideas, as the appendix to the proposal made clear with numerous newspaper clippings. But BRL had never put all these ideas together in one school before.

BRL was not unique in this regard. Rand reports that *every* performance contract it studied took several weeks to several months before it operated as originally designed.

It took time to implement the changes in instruction even within the program, since all of the "learning systems" had to be tailored to fit the many different variables in specific districts. Some of the programs did not become fully implemented until almost half of the year was gone. (32)

At Banneker, it took that full half-year to approach the broad outline of what was originally intended. By the third year of the project, however, Banneker will have a system at least as sophisticated as the system outlined in the proposal.

An inconsistency exists, of course, between the implicit assumption behind the performance contract idea—that someone can do instantaneously what needs to be done—and the fact that developmental time and effort were needed. In those heady weeks in the spring of 1970 when performance contracts seemed such a good idea, not much attention was given to the nitty gritty of doing this new thing. As McAndrew put it, "We didn't really build in enough provision for development input." (33) The entire summer of 1971, in fact, BRL devoted to developmental efforts which had not even been envisioned prior to the project.

Writing the Contract Document

Writing the contract itself proved very difficult. Sandra Irons, then vice-president of the Gary Teachers Union, said she saw twenty-two drafts of the contract during the summer of 1970. (34) In one sense, the contract was a formality, since agreement had been reached in principle and efforts were well underway to begin the program. BRL and Gary chose the school, chose the staff, hired an evaluator, chose the management, conducted preservice training and began the school year before the contract was finally signed September 22, 1970.

There were obvious difficulties. With no real precedent for either BRL or Gary, the contract had to be created out of whole cloth. With an unclear image of the actual project in the minds of either party, specification of details often proved impossible. Also there were many publics to satisfy: the union would examine the BRL contract in terms of its own; the staff, the board, the press and other educators would subsequently examine it; and BRL especially would use it for public relations purposes.

The most serious difficulty, however, was with the State of Indiana. The project was treading on untried legal ground, and Superintendent Wells made no secret that he would oppose the project on legal grounds. (Privately, Wells also tried to halt the project by offering an alternative, in August, 1970: $20,000 "no strings attached" to hire a BRL consultant. This was unknown until Wells himself announced it at the February, 1971, State Board of Education meeting.)

The BRL proposal called for Gary to subcontract the entire school thereby giving BRL a free reign. During the summer, this procedure was challenged informally by the state. The view taken by the State Department of Public Instruction was that Banneker was part of the state school system subject to all the state laws and regulations as administered by the state superintendent, the local school board, and other state agencies. In short, the Gary board could not subcontract its responsibility to operate Banneker School.

Therefore, the version of the contract signed September 22nd, retroactive to July 1, 1970, makes BRL "consultants to assist in establishing a school . . . under the supervision and control of the board" and to "recommend plans and assist in their implementation." (35) The BRL proposal was referred to as "a proposal for consultation and guidance" and it was noted that the project "must be implemented solely through and in accordance with applicable Indiana statutes and duly adopted regulations relating among other things to curriculum, licensing of teachers, and purchase of supplies." (36)

According to a union spokesman the contract provided that BRL would serve as consultant, yet in fact BRL controlled the operation of the school. John Hand, reporting to the Indiana Board of Education in January, said,

"Although the contract . . . contains various disclaimers and clauses which purportedly limit BRL to a consultative function and vest ultimate control of the program in the School City, the actual operation does not differ in any substantial way from the original proposal." (37)

The Banneker contract is a blanket contract. That is, first the agreement was reached, then a contract which substantially covered the agreement was written. So far as anyone in Gary could tell this author, very little use was made of the contract document itself; Gary and BRL proceeded on the basis of mutual good will, not by the letter of the contract. From the union's vantage point, this cavalier attitude toward the device of contracting was just the reverse of its relationship with the Gary schools, where resorting to the letter of their agreement had replaced mutual good will.

Conclusion

By the time Banneker School opened its doors for teacher training in August and for students in September, what had begun a few months earlier as an idea between a school superintendent and a corporate president of similar disposition had mushroomed into a controversial educational project of national interest with racial, political, and educational implications which reached far beyond Gary: a private corporation was going to manage a public school—a black school with underachieving students—and had guaranteed to achieve impressive learning gains for students.

Goals for that school had been specified, in terms of test scores, and BRL was committed to create an instructional system that would strive for those goals.

Banneker had already passed through several political skirmishes with the stage set for several more. Locally and nationally, teacher organizations had vehemently opposed the project. Locally and nationally, partisans for the program had underestimated the difficulty and overestimated BRL's readiness to fulfill its guarantee.

All this under the umbrella of a new, dramatic, ill-understood phenomenon called "performance contracting" which had strong advocates in Washington but had suddenly acquired a dubious reputation after scandal clouded the first performance contract in Texarkana.

Notes

(1) Rand Corporation accepted a $300,000 grant to study performance contracts during 1970-1971 and produce three documents. The first, J. P. Stucker and G. R. Hall, *The Performance Contracting Concept in Education* (Santa Monica: Rand, 1971), dealt with theory. The second was a six-volume report containing five case studies and one summary volume:
   Case Studies in Educational Performance Contracting (Santa Monica: Rand, 1971).
      Volume 1, P. Carpenter and G. R. Hall, *Conclusions and Implications,*
      Volume 2, P. Carpenter, *Norfolk, Virginia,*
      Volume 3, P. Carpenter; A. W. Chalfant; and G. R. Hall, *Texarkana, Arkansas and Liberty Eylau, Texas,*
      Volume 4, G. R. Hall and M. L. Rapp, *Gary, Indiana,*
      Volume 5, M. L. Rapp and G. R. Hall, *Gilroy, California,*
      Volume 6, G. C. Sumner, *Grant Rapids, Michigan.*
   The third document is to be a guide intended for use by educational officials.
(2) Carpenter and Hall, *Case Studies,* Vol. 1, p. vii.

(3) "Teaching for Profit," *Newsweek,* August 17, 1970. Copyright Newsweek, Inc., 1970.

(4) For example, in 1971, the school board adopted businesslike nomenclature. The superintendent became "president," the staff became vice-presidents, etc.

(5) *Education Turnkey News,* 1 (September 1970): 2.

(6) Personal letter written by Gordon McAndrew to the Experimental Schools Program of the U. S. Office of Education, May 12, 1971.

(7) This author and John A. Wilson held an interview with Charles Smith at Gary, Indiana, December 19, 1970.

(8) Stated by Gordon McAndrew in an interview with the author and John A. Wilson, at Gary, Indiana, January 11, 1971.

(9) J. Poppy, "Sullivan's Crusade: Schools Without Pain," *Look,* 30 (June 28, 1966): 38-39.

(10) The gross income of BRL for fiscal 1970 exceeded $10 million, up $3 million from 1969. Gross income for fiscal 1971 exceeded $13 million. Comparing the projected $640,000 (800 students × $800) to be received by BRL during 1970-1971, gross income from Banneker would be less than 5 percent of the gross income for BRL.

(11) M. Anderson, "Private Company Runs a Public School to Boost Kids' Learning," *The National Observer,* October 26, 1970, citing an interview with George Stern. Reprinted with permission from *The National Observer,* copyright Dow, Jones & Company, Inc.

(12) Stated by Gordon McAndrew in an interview with the author and John A. Wilson, at Gary, Indiana, January 11, 1971.

(13) Ibid.

(14) Stated by Theodore Nering in an interview with the author and John A. Wilson, at Gary, Indiana, January 11, 1971.

(15) "Performance Contracting: Why the Gary School Board Bought It, And How," *American School Board Journal,* 158 (January 1971): 19-21, citing an interview with Alphonso Holliday.

(16) Behavioral Research Laboratories, "A Proposal for a Performance Contracted Curriculum Center Under the Right To Learn Program of the School City of Gary, Indiana," submitted by Behavioral Research Laboratories to the School City of Gary, Indiana, June 1, 1970, citing Gordon McAndrew's introductory remarks to the Proposal.

(17) Behavioral Research Laboratories, "A Proposal for a Performance Contracted Curriculum Center."

(18) Ibid.

(19) Stated by Otha Porter in an interview with Orest Ochitwa in Gary, Indiana, October, 1970.

(20) "Performance Contracting: Why the Gary School Board Bought It. And How," *American School Board Journal,* 158 (January 1971): 21, citing an interview with Alphonso Holliday.

(21) A. H. Malcolm, "Company to Teach Gary, Ind. Pupils," *The New York Times,* July 26, 1970, p. 56, citing an interview with Clarence Benford. ©1970 by The New York Times Company. Reprinted by permission.

(22) Anderson, "Private Company Runs a Public School," citing an interview with Gordon McAndrew.

(23) "School City of Gary Reports Success at Banneker Elementary School," a press release from School City of Gary, September 29, 1971.

(24) Stated by George Wood, principal of Aetna Elementary School in Gary, in an interview with the author and John A. Wilson, November, 1970.

(25) G. McAndrew, "Why Banneker?" *Superintendent's Newsletter,* October 30, 1970.

(26) Stated by Gordon McAndrew in a January 11, 1971, interview.

(27) Behavioral Research Laboratories, "A Proposal for a Performance Contracted Curriculum Center."

(28) Carpenter and Hall, Case Studies, Vol. 1, p. 39.

(29) Behavioral Research Laboratories, "A Proposal for a Performance Contracted Curriculum Center."

(30) Ibid.

(31) Ibid.

(32) P. Carpenter, "An Evaluation of Performance Contracting for HEW," conference paper delivered at the National Conference on Performance Contracting, Elkridge, Maryland, December 9, 1971, p. ix.

(33) Stated by Gordon McAndrew in an interview with the author and John A. Wilson, at Gary, Indiana, May, 1971.
(34) Stated by Sandra Irons in her address to the Truth and Soul in Teaching Conference of the American Federation of Teachers, Chicago, Illinois, January 16, 1971.
(35) Hall and Rapp, *Case Studies,* Vol. 4, p. 96.
(36) Ibid.
(37) John S. Hand, Memo to the State Board of Education re "Banneker Elementary School, Gary, Indiana," January 11, 1971.

IV

The First Year of Banneker

News Management
in Performance Contracting

Performance contracting is ripe for satire, although people regard the movement so seriously that there has not been much. One piece, "Promises, Promises", struck at guarantees, concluding "the author prefers to bid on the treasury and promise a balanced budget, lower taxes, and a reduced national debt. He will get 2 percent if he succeeds and 1 percent if he does not." (1)

The most quoted satirical article is by Gary Saretsky who parodied Lessinger's *Every Kid a Winner* with "Every Kid a Hustler." He explains how students can hustle the contractor whose final payment depends upon the students doing well on tests. (2)

In "Performance Contracting in the Year of the News Release" (3) Saretsky struck at the Achilles heel; for most of what outsiders know about Banneker and many other performance contracts comes from carefully engineered press releases.

The national experiment of the Office of Economic Opportunity, for example, in the name of rigorous experimentation swore everyone involved to secrecy. Thus, all year, OEO issued rosy stories about its projects while people working in them were silent.

News management is understandable; nobody wants to issue uncomplimentary data about himself. But as Peter Schrag asserts, it runs counter to the public's "right to know;" he says the public *generally* cannot get accurate information about city schools, not just in regard to performance contracts. "The local press," says Schrag, "through inadequate resources, or innocence, or sheer incompetence, becomes a public relations tool of the system, reporting the statements of 'official' leaders. . . ." (4)

News Management at Banneker

Schrag's comments should be inverted for Gary. Ernie Hernandez, writing for the *Gary Post-Tribune,* stayed close to events at Banneker while newspapers and news media in Chicago, Washington, New York, and elsewhere parroted the press releases. (At one point, Gary bypassed Hernandez entirely and gave a story about good test score results exclusively to the Chicago Sun-Times. (5)

Banneker faced serious problems its first semester. For whatever reasons—fear, pride, certainty the problems would quickly disappear—Gary administrators kept these problems from the press. When these stories did break in the *Post-Tribune* just before Christmas, they "shocked the Gary community, which has believed all was well at Banneker." (6) Until *Newsweek* published "Banneker at Bay" in March, 1971, (7) and *Phi Delta Kappan* published "The Performance Contract in Gary" (8) the same month, neither the national media nor the educational press reported any problems at Banneker except the mid-winter confrontation with the Indiana State Department of Public Instruction.

The Narrow Curriculum

Instead, national coverage was given to a press release September 29th and to a "fact sheet" issued October 2nd. Neither document spoke of problems; both documents radiated enthusiasm. And each document described Banneker as if the BRL proposal had already been implemented, although it had not been:

The Banneker Elementary School has been transformed into a nongraded center, where the students attend courses in five curriculum areas—language arts, mathematics, social studies, and foreign languages, science and enrichment—including arts and crafts, music, drama and physical education. (9)

Report cards were not issued at Banneker until early December, which for many parents was the first time they had realized Banneker was only teaching reading and mathematics. What of science, social studies and enrichment, they asked. Donald Kendrick, the BRL Center manager, offered the explanation that "the materials are coming and that the subjects not taught now will be taught." (10)

McAndrew said months later,

We made the decision to phase in the components and it was my feeling that we could phase them in between September and January. . . . The original contract called for the five instructional areas, so there was never any intention of just having reading and math. (11)

Nevertheless, when the reading-and-math-only story broke, it was grist for the critics' mill. They said that since BRL was to be paid only on the basis of reading and mathematics gains, that's all BRL taught.

Also, the talk of mechanistic "dehumanized" teaching that had first greeted the project surfaced again.

Leadership Crisis

But the narrow curriculum was only one of several problems. A second was the crisis over leadership. According to the contract, the leadership would be split: BRL would supply a Center manager who will cooperate in directing the organization and non-academic affairs of the school and Gary would supply a learning director who shall have the status of a principal. No further attention was paid to defining these roles.

Clarence Benford, who had been the principal of Banneker in 1968, was reassigned there for 1970. When Banneker subsequently was chosen for the BRL-Gary contract, Benford became "learning director." Donald Kendrick was a "systems analyst"; his previous experience had been with Lockheed, where from 1967 to 1969 he had been in "Operations Research, Education Systems," according to his vita. (12) Kendrick lacked the credentials to be certified in Indiana as a school administrator; consequently the Banneker contract says the Center manager will merely cooperate in directing the organization and nonacademic affairs of the school.

From the beginning, however, administrative duties did not divide as the contract might suggest. Benford, after all, did not know the BRL materials, as Kendrick did. Benford was not familiar with individualized instruction systems nor with "systems approaches" in general; he lacked the training or experience to direct learning as it needed to be done under the BRL proposal. Moreover, because the agreement between Gary and BRL had been to subcontract the school (until the State of Indiana intervened), BRL had the mandate, the "clout", at Banneker. Nothing in the situation encouraged the learning director to exert authority. Benford, feeling outflanked by Kendrick and his staff of aides and consultants, did not exert any.

Otha Porter, official Gary liaison to the project, both a close friend of Benford and a strong supporter of Banneker, found himself trying to soothe the situation as well as to rationalize it. He saw it this way:

It's a human problem. Here I am, I've been a school principal for thirteen years. As a school principal I am king of all I survey, in terms of school concerns in my district. When school city or any group signs a contract or an agreement with a company, and we're talking about funds—profit and loss—you must give the company representative certain leeway lest the contract is no longer valid. Consequently the principal—or the former principal—must assume an entirely new role.

He assumes a role, say, of an assistant principal in a sense, in terms of actual performance in a school. Then when you consider the financial arrangement, where people might be up tight in terms of the progress of the pupil, and you're talking about millions of dollars now, you must be careful how you manage the relationship with the company person in that particular case. The agreement is with the company. (13)

From the perspective of teachers at Banneker, who had known and liked Benford in previous years, it seemed as if Benford had been stepped upon. Weeks of squabbling, jockeying, and hurt feelings affected the morale of the school, causing teachers to choose sides or perhaps to question their own decision to work at Banneker. Half the teachers made it known they might resign. Leadership at Banneker was the touchiest topic of the first semester. When asked how the contractual division of leadership had been implemented, everyone changed the subject; they did not want to air *this* conflict in the press. Such a story would suggest that schools and private companies could not get along—and, after the claims made for performance contracting, Gary and BRL did not need that kind of publicity.

Finally, Ernie Hernandez reported the conflict:

The principal, Clarence Benford, was eased out of control by designating him "learning director" in charge of the educational approaches of Banneker. Observers note, however, that Kendrick emerged as controller of all aspects of the school. (14)

In Hammond, Indiana, where OEO had one of its eighteen performance contracts, the contractor used no certified teachers in his learning center; nevertheless, to satisfy accreditation requirements, one certified teacher was assigned there to supervise instruction. (15) Benford's role in December was similar. John Hand, the chief state investigator, reported to the Indiana State Board of Education, January 11, 1971, that Benford exercised none of the twenty administrative duties designated by regulations as those of elementary school principals:

The *de facto* building administrator at Banneker School is Donald Kendrick. . . . Benford does not perform even those functions that are specifically assigned to him in the BRL contract. Although he is designated Learning Director, Benford makes no instructional or curricular decisions or assignments. (16)

After the January and February meetings of the Indiana Board, Benford acquired more and more of those twenty administrative duties. Otha Porter said in February that Kendrick's role had been reduced to that of a "mighty powerful consultant." (17)

This leadership problem was not just a matter of personalities, although some have chosen to understand it that way. Performance contracting alters the customary relationships of power and authority in a school. In Banneker, despite this fundamental change, no attention was paid to the transition. With Kendrick's sizeable staff of assistants; with George Stern and other BRL executives appearing at Banneker frequently; with Gordon McAndrew, Otha Porter and other central staff in and out daily, and many BRL consultants in and out, no one knew who was in charge or where the buck stopped.

Not until the second year was there a tolerable solution. Then Gary and BRL each selected new individuals for Banneker's twin leadership whose styles are more complementary and who liked each other. As Banneker settled down in the spring, BRL and Gary executives appeared at Banneker less frequently, so that the team of Brian Fitch as Center manager and Sherman Newell as learning director became the leaders. Banneker had not really resolved the question of authority but merely had managed to table it.

Semantic Confusion

A third problem, closely related but quite distinct, is the problem of the language of change. "Performance contract" and "guarantee" were new terms to education, but useful ones because they had a familiar and attractive ring. In the name of these things, genuine change could be made to occur; they were excellent "soft revolutionary" terms, useful for making "changes in the way things are done, profound changes, if possible." (18) Generally, McAndrew uses such terms well, minimizing use of language that will antagonize. But others involved in Banneker were not so tactful, choosing at times to use language (and behavior) that antagonized people unnecessarily.

"What we have here is a system integration problem" Kendrick told interviewers in October, 1970. (19) Kendrick was correct; Banneker represents a system integration problem. But the use of such terminology was not helpful because teachers generally do not respond well to it. He told another visitor in December,

I'm a systems analyst. I view things analytically. Keep out emotions. Industry says we want a job done. This is the difference (between industry and schools). You don't have to love the guy next to you on the assembly line to make the product. He puts in the nuts, you put in the bolts, and the product comes out. Teachers can hate me and still get children to learn. (20)

Kendrick told a *Wall Street Journal* reporter,

This project is like building a missile. Every child is a component: you have to keep an eye on each one to see how he's functioning. We start with the basic assumption that any child can learn and that if he doesn't something must be wrong with the system. (21)

That schools must set workable goals, in terms of student learning, and accept responsibility for achieving them—these are sentiments that, when properly phrased, will appeal to educators. Not the ideas, but the industry / missile / component / functioning / assembly line / nuts and bolts images, served to alienate teachers. Too many people responded as did Francine Moscove, a teacher in Roosevelt High School in Gary. Her pamphlet, "The Experiment at Banneker School," published May, 1971 by a local writers workshop (22) received wide circulation in Gary and was quoted extensively in the

Gary Post-Tribune. After quoting Kendrick for two pages of her pamphlet, she said:

The goals and values of the company were reflected in the people who are chosen to represent it . . . Mr. Kendrick's attitudes are those of a man who wants a job done and damn the consequences. The consequences of this kind of an attitude are all too apparent. Industry's lack of interest in the by-products of its production techniques is appalling. Here we see that the focus is on the output of the system and the by-product of human hostility is considered irrelevant. Since the children are viewed as a "product" with no human response system, it is assumed that it does not matter that the people who "put in the nuts and bolts" are hostile toward the system, and each other. . . . It seems that we adult humans are to become automatons on an assembly line conveyor belt down which roll our children. We need only to take orders, put in the nuts and bolts, ignore each other, and our children will come rolling off the conveyor belt like so many pieces of assembled machinery. (23)

Mrs. Moscove never visited Banneker. The language of its spokesmen seemed sufficient to her; her pamphlet attempted "to analyze the consequences of corporate involvement in school planning and administration" based largely upon the imagery employed. (24)

Yet the same ideas, in different language, can appeal to teachers. For example, they were proposed in 1970 by a study committee of the American Federation of Teachers as new guidelines for the showcase More Effective Schools:

1) The supportive services must exist, but only under the umbrella of a total instructional process. In other words, the supportive staff must be subservient to the process of instruction.

2) The instructional process must be defined in workable, measurable and viable terms. . . . This process includes five components: behavioral objectives, diagnosis, prescription, instruction, and assessment.

. . . . . .

7) The cluster structure (staffing pattern), the heart of the MES program, must be revamped. The entire concept of the cluster should be defined in terms of its usefulness to the MES. (25)

Banneker in December

Among many familiar with the project there was strong feeling in December, 1970, that Banneker had been disappointing, or worse. The bold promises of the previous spring, which had been reiterated in public statements all year, had been replaced by frustration felt by union officials, several parents, some board members, and some teachers. The Center for Urban Redevelopment and Education (CURE) served as an outside evaluator of the Banneker project. Its obligation was to monitor the project and make bi-monthly reports. Otha Porter remarked at the State Board of Education meeting

January 19 that every criticism raised by the State he had heard from CURE the month before and had been working since Christmas to correct.

Some observers and some advocates of performance contracting with learning companies claim that "outsiders" are more flexible, more able to change, more able to admit mistakes, more free from bureaucratic constraints than are school administrators. "Outsiders appear to be freer," according to RAND. (26) "What BRL can do," said BRL president George Stern, "is to get things done rapidly, differently and effectively, to evaluate unfavorable situations and to correct them in a hurry." (27)

This is what happened at Banneker from December to June of the first year. January and February were tumultuous. Union and State of Indiana conflicts peaked simultaneously, while at Banneker major changes determined during Christmas vacation were accelerated to satisfy these critics.

Conflict with
the State and Union

Both the conflict with the Gary Teachers Union and that with the State Department of Public Instruction seem less critical in retrospect than they did as they were occurring. At that time, reading the *Gary Post-Tribune* and attending the State Board of Education meetings, one could not know for sure whether Banneker would survive. In terms of killing Banneker, both the union and the State won on points at the time but lost the match. Banneker emerged from the fray a better project than before and more secure. No doubt, these conflicts brought public scrutiny to the project, highlighted its flaws, and accelerated their correction. For State Superintendent Richard Wells and for the AFT leadership, however, this salutary outcome was decidedly second-best. (28)

From the beginning, the Gary Teachers Union had opposed Banneker for what seemed clear violations of the union contract; similarly, the State opposed Banneker for several violations of regulations. Both objected to Banneker politically as well.

After the contract was signed in September, the union unsuccessfully raised its objections to the Gary school board. Then the union threatened to strike unless it received redress over violations of contract or unless these violations were submitted to binding arbitration. There were three issues. First, fourteen teachers had been transferred from Banneker during August. This action antagonized the union, for in Gary building seniority is prized. Second, after reducing the certified teaching staff, BRL hired twenty aides—mothers from the community—and paired one with each teacher as a teaching team; the union objected that the teacher-pupil ratio had suddenly jumped to over 40:1, which exceeded the maximum class size in the union contract. Third, the Banneker contract contains a clause which requires Gary to transfer any teacher on 15-day written notice from BRL; this too was taken as violation of contract.

The union voted 476–376 to strike, which out of 2000 members was not a strong response. Subsequently, at school board insistence, the union agreed to follow its grievance procedure.

Simultaneously, the Indiana Board of Education had five official objections: 1) that the exclusive teaching of reading and mathematics had violated regulations concerning time allocations in the curriculum; 2) that the BRL textbooks were not on the state adopted list, nor had the proper waiver been requested; 3) Kendrick was performing administrative duties for which he was not certified; 4) some teachers were improperly certified; and 5) the pupil-teacher ratio exceeded state-mandated maximum.

In addition, politically, professionally and emotionally, both the state and the union shared other concerns: they worried about the quality of the Banneker educational program; they worried that performance contracting might spread to other schools in Gary and Indiana, at their expense; they were angered that Gary had disregarded state regulations and its union contract; and they were annoyed that each had received poor publicity from some quarters—both union and state officials believed they had been unfairly stereotyped as mossbacked defenders of the *status quo*.

Because state and union concerns overlapped, the union chose to let the state take the lead in prosecuting Banneker. For its own sake, the union could not afford to antagonize the black community of Gary which favors the program strongly. The month-long strike the year before had already spurred bitter anti-union feelings, feelings reinforced by the perception that the union is a white-dominated organization.

At the State Board meeting in January, a motion to "decommission" Banneker school was narrowly defeated 8 to 6. Decommissioning would have dropped Banneker from the state school system and thereby disqualified it from receiving state monies. Instead, Banneker was given a month's probation to conform to state regulations.

John Hand, the state investigator, reported in February that an effort had been made to meet the state's objections. Teachers had been certified, Benford restored to some administrative duties, several curriculum areas "phased in" and teacher-pupil ratio reduced. Clarence Benford remarked some months later that the school did not really begin to operate to everyone's satisfaction until February. (29) Because of rapid improvement at Banneker, observers close to the State Board would not predict prior to the meeting how the State Board might vote.

However, political considerations outweighed improvement at

Banneker. As punishment for Gary's disregard of law and regulation, as a sign that private corporations were not welcome in public schools in Indiana, as proof that the Board was true to its word, and in support of Superintendent Wells' desires, the Board voted to decommission Banneker. Some hoped their decommissioning of Banneker would force BRL to pack up and go back to California.

Meanwhile, the American Arbitration Association designated an arbitrator between the Gary board of education and the union. In the procedure for selecting an arbitrator the board and union had each ranked acceptable candidates. The arbitrator designated by the Association was John Sembower—the union's first choice, but the board's sixth choice. Claiming this was patently unfair, the board refused to attend the arbitration hearing. Although "in 45 years of administering labor-management arbitrations the AAA has never had such an objection," (30) the board remained adamant even when the meeting was postponed to give them a chance to reconsider. Although the arbitrator announced in late February that he concurred with the union's grievance, the school board refused to act on his "advisory" recommendations. Ernie Hernandez, in "Teachers' Union Won—Or Did It?" noted that:

The Gary Teachers Union is finding out that an arbitrator's decision is hardly enough to turn things around at the controversial Banneker School. . . . Charles O. Smith . . . said that he "expects" the school board, headed by Alphonso D. Holliday II, to abide by Sembower's five-point decision. Yet it is clear that "expecting" is about all his union can do about the decision. (31)

By March, Banneker had resolved all Indiana's official objections. BRL added slightly to the Banneker staff, enrollment dropped slightly also, and some BRL personnel were certified; together these changes relieved the teacher-pupil ratio. Clarence Benford acquired more administrative duties; more important, BRL was in the process of hiring a certifiable individual as Center manager. Banneker was recommissioned. As a face-saving measure, the State Board made its commission "probationary" although no one reexamined the school the following year.

Significance of the Conflicts

Probably no one, throughout these state and union conflicts, tried to sympathize with Banneker, to understand its problems on its own terms, or to excuse its faults on the basis that the program at Banneker was developmental. Instead, both state and union agreed that BRL and Gary did not conform to expectations—those written in law as well as those written in the BRL proposal. There is this irony: Banneker, which as a "performance" contract asked to be judged on ultimate performance, was judged instead on its process. As George Stern understood it,

The union and later the state Department of Education would have taken the guts out of the program and invalidated the entire thing. What they wanted to do was to achieve the objectives without making any changes. It would have been the old system again and it would have had as much of a chance to succeed as the old system had, which was not much. (32)

A crucial issue raised by Banneker, pertinent not only to other performance contracts but to educational innovation generally, is the role of law and regulations vis-a-vis change. Banneker, after all, was decommissioned because Gary had not "fully conformed to the rules and regulations of the State Board of Education." (33) That same day, the State Board unanimously approved a resolution favoring all educational innovations that will benefit children provided only that they conform to regulations. During that meeting some members of the board repeatedly asserted that Gary had behaved illegally, shamefully and immorally; they were convinced that the Banneker program should be scuttled for this reason, as a lesson to Gary and others.

Are there circumstances which justify disregarding laws and regulations? Like George Stern, many who advocate change, including performance contracts, believe there are reasons. "It takes a school board with a lot of *guts* to do some of the things that you think should be done, because you're locked in by laws and agreements!", (34) Otha Porter told a conference of the Indiana School Board Association. Responding to Porter at the same meeting, Charles Blaschke expanded on the point:

First of all, I think we're in sad shape in education when we let lawyers determine educational policy. I think the legal profession, especially in education, is a long way behind. . . . Law is not the great formulator of social justice or reform; it holds on to the past.

I think every performance contract project that I have been involved in has been illegal. There were seventeen laws we broke in Texarkana. God knows how many others!

Law in education, today, is in a new formation stage. There are lots of shibboleths and myths and customs and traditions and regulations, but in terms of good precedent law, there isn't that much. Yes, we're going to have some legal problems. But instead of lawyers who tell you twenty-five reasons why you can't do something, seek someone who will tell you, "Here's a way you might be able to do it." (35)

Changing Emphasis at Banneker

What Kendrick had once called a "system *integration* problem"—putting together various ideas and materials (components) into a systematic school—his replacement, Brian Fitch, portrayed as a "system *development* problem." "Let's talk straightforwardly," he said:

People who enter into this kind of operation have to realize the magnitude of the project they are undertaking, and that you don't merely come in and in a short period of time get the thing set up all at once.

No independent outfit is simply going to come in and drop a system onto a school.

I think, realistically, that the host school system should realize the staff in the school that is in the performance contract is going to have to work very very hard in helping to develop that program. (36)

Fitch arrived at Banneker in April, shortly after the school had been recommissioned. BRL had hired him especially for Banneker; until then he had been working at the Upper Midwest Regional Educational Laboratory, in Minneapolis, developing individualized instructional systems. Banneker was "right along the lines of what I was working on before," he said, "so this was very appealing." (37)

For many reasons, Fitch proved an excellent choice. Most critically, he held a doctorate in educational administration, which made him certifiable in Indiana.

Second, young, flexible, knowledgeable, respectful of BRL's efforts and materials but willing to criticize, quiet in demeanor, conversant in the language of teachers and schools, Fitch struck a soft, accepting, warm pose that suited the moment.

Third, Fitch acquired teacher support. For two months, he observed, listened, asked questions, and responded to questions. During the crisis months at Banneker, teachers had stepped into a management role and taken upon themselves more decision-making authority. According to Rand:

The curriculum managers also came to be regarded as part of the top management and assumed considerable authority. The five curriculum managers make up the Curriculum Committee, which is a management group. As of the spring of 1971 it deliberated on and passed on practically every school decision. To an outsider it seemed that many of the matters they considered might appropriately have been delegated to the learning director or center manager. Apparently, however, a feeling that they were neglected in the fall has led the curriculum managers to resist any delegation. (38)

In this circumstance, another autocratic leader at Banneker would have been inappropriate, and Fitch chose instead to lead by consensus. Fitch listened to teacher advice, and chose to act upon it. By late spring, teachers expressed a cautious optimism about Fitch, would confide in him, advise him, and assist him.

Fourth, Fitch pleased Gary administrators. Inevitably, as school system officials had found themselves devoting days of their own time to defending and troubleshooting Banneker, their control had increased and the BRL "clout" had waned. By spring, "The authority of McAndrew, Battle, Porter, and Benford over the program was no longer in doubt." (39) While Gary did not wish to regain all control from BRL, the events of the first year made it necessary for Gary to feel assured, by BRL, that subsequent years would improve. Fitch, whose professional commitment is toward the improvement of schooling by applying "systems approaches" to schools, personified that assurance. Moreover, Fitch and Kendrick, with McAndrew's support, received authorization from BRL to initiate "a substantial amount of developmental activity" (40) over the summer, at an estimated cost of BRL of $50,000 or more, which demonstrated the BRL commitment to changes at Banneker.

Finally, Fitch had a knack for explaining the presence of himself and BRL, he cut through the now uncomfortable promises and hyperbole surrounding Banneker. He enabled people to reaffirm their original decision to contract with BRL. He said:

The performance contract really provides a basis for negotiations between independent systems developers and school people.

People in regular school systems have been going along for a lot of years here, trying to do a job in the schools. And as with any job that somebody tries to do, some of it's been done well and some of it has been bad. What people are saying now is, in order to do something better we've got to find some new techniques in the area.

Who's on top of new techniques? It doesn't seem to be people who are already in the school systems, as hard as they've been working. The people with the new techniques seem to be people who have come from outside the general education thing: they are people who have been trained up in industry, or who have taken highly specialized degrees in education that have given them a lot of work in "ed. psych.", and in curriculum and materials development, and systems analysis.

You want to bring in some people with special expertise, hopefully people who know something about school systems and something about how education has run in the past (so that you don't just run head-on into the establishment and get all hung-up in that kind of a fight).

You've got to remember, too, that BRL—this is one of the things that attracts me to BRL—BRL has been working for a long time on individualized systems in reading. They've just developed one in math. They've put a lot of time and their money into developing these. They've had a lot of experience in other schools. So these people already have a leg up on this systems development business. They've developed systems.

Gary could have gone to Minnesota and hired me. But they couldn't have hired that kind of expertise, that kind of developmental knowledge, that kind of experience. BRL, as a company, is able to supply a lot of support, in addition to people like myself. (41)

Visitors to Banneker in late spring found the school a sharp contrast from Christmastime. Where once visitation had been restricted or closely guarded, visitors now roamed freely. Where once people were tightlipped about problems at Banneker, now problems were aired and compared to changes being made. Where once teachers and students radiated tension, now an ease in their manner bespoke inner confidence and pleasure.

Where the *Gary Post-Tribune* had reported the school as a rat's nest of conflict and confusion at Christmastime, in June reporter Mary Ann Curtis "was given carte blanche to observe, hear, inquire, and ask any question that came to mind." (42) She first listed her initial doubts about Banneker, reiterated the conflicts of the first year and the stories she had heard. But her visit cast her doubts aside and her June 6th article was nearly solid praise. Capping that praise, she echoed what had become a new theme in discussion of Banneker:

Possibly the most exciting thing that has happened has been the fresh enthusiasm evidenced in many of the teachers. As one said, "It is thrilling to see how our teachers have grown. I'm proud to be one of them. If we have been able to do this much in this first confusing year, imagine the great hopes we have for the years to come! (43)

Gordon McAndrew was equally impressed by the change in teachers at Banneker. He said in August that the fact that "a pretty representative cross-section" of Gary teachers had assumed responsibility at Banneker was "extremely encouraging" and "one of the most significant things" that had occurred. (44) Teachers said the same; for example, "Banneker is going to be a team effort; I think the teachers have really held that school together." (45)

Neither BRL nor Fitch can claim the major credit for causing a growing teacher esprit. Probably the teachers' perception that the union and the State of Indiana had fought on their side was more directly responsible. However one must credit Fitch (and BRL for selecting and supporting him) for encouraging this change and emphasizing the importance of teachers at Banneker.

In a memo to the curriculum managers (teachers) dated May 18th, Fitch prefaced a lengthy summary of plans for development with these personal remarks to teachers:

Attached is a description of the kinds of steps which should be taken to improve the program at Banneker. What I have written reflects your statements about the program, what I have observed, and where I think we can go from where we are now.

Please feel free to criticize constructively and to make suggestions. The attached paper is very general. We will get much more specific in committee meetings as we work together to plan our development program. WE ALL NEED TO SHARE OUR IDEAS AND TO WORK TOGETHER! Our goal must be to provide an increasingly better program for each learner and to make it easier for teachers to manage that program. . . . I'm looking forward to your comments and reactions. (46)

In sum, when Banneker began in 1970, it was perceived by everyone involved as *primarily a demonstration*. Subsequent events revealed that these early perceptions had been premature; Banneker had first to become *primarily a development project*.

With this shift in emphasis, the energetic implementor (Kendrick) was replaced by a quiet facilitator (Fitch). Teachers, who had been ignored, became vital participants in managing the school. Gary administrators, who had at first given BRL free rein, were sharing in decision making. In summer, 1971, Banneker was, for all intents and purposes, a new project. The dramatic performance contract "hooplah" that had been so integral at the beginning of the program no longer fit the situation (although, as shall be seen, it was maintained in the press).

It was as if those who had bet against Phileas Fogg in this trip around the world later decided to aid him to win his bet.

Pedagogy and Standardized Testing

Performance contracting is not a pedagogical technique. Many pedagogies have been employed under performance contracts or could be. However, many who have written about Banneker and other performance contracts have visited projects and then emphasized the staffing patterns, textbooks, programmed instruction, individualized instruction, diagnostic testing, changes in scheduling, use of teaching machines, and other techniques which have been employed because of performance contracting.

What is new about performance contracting, and highly visible at Banneker, is 1) the link between money and learning, with the drama that results, 2) stress upon desired outcomes of schooling, 3) new relationships between school districts and subcontractors, 4) changed roles for administrators and others, 5) unique legal and morale problems, and 6) the rapidity with which changes occur. Performance contracting also calls attention to the politics of education.

Therefore, in this book very little is said about the pedagogy employed at Banneker, neither what was intended, what actually occurred, nor how Brian Fitch proceeded to change it. For this the reader is referred to other sources. (47) But one aspect of pedagogy cannot be separated from performance contracting (at least, historically) nor from its politics, and that is the heavy reliance on standardized testing. For in virtually every performance contract during the first two years, standardized tests of academic achievement provided the measure of contractors' success or failure.

What frequently happened in performance contracts, as at Banneker, was that the educational purpose of the project—to experiment with methods to improve teaching and learning—was publicly expressed as raising test scores. BRL guaranteed certain test scores, or it would refund the money received. One astute reporter phrased it, "Gary's 'Accountability' School—Where Test Scores Mean Money." (48)

The first question raised about the use of tests in performance contracts is the temptation of contractors to "teach the test." Partly as a consequence of the Texarkana experience, the Gary contract contains provisions to avoid teaching the test: the outside evaluator was to examine the teaching materials and certify that the BRL materials did not duplicate the Metropolitan Achievement test.

Second, questions have frequently surfaced over the administration of the tests. Hasty, untrained test administrators, poor testing situations, absent and transient students, improper test security—all these problems have cropped up again and again concerning performance contracts, especially in the fall pretests. The OEO national experiment was particularly prone to these problems; but several of the same problems were reported by observers of testing at Banneker.

A third question, usually rhetorical, asked, "Is it appropriate to turn test scores into goals of schooling?" About this, some become very defensive. As one Gary administrator confided,

In fact, for better or worse or right or wrong, that's the way we do it! We let kids into college based on the SAT, and we let them into graduate school based on the Miller Analogy, and we let them into industry based on all kinds of standardized tests. (49)

A fourth question examines validity of these tests when used in performance contracts; a related question deals with reliability and precision of the data collected. During 1970-1971, many of the nation's leading testing and evaluation experts published criticisms of the testing done in performance contracting. These experts concur, over-all, that standardized tests are not precise instruments, that they have been inappropriately selected and applied in most performance contracts and for this reason they yield highly suspect data which are prone to misinterpretation. (50)

Most contracts, including the Gary contract, have assumed the metaphor of each individual students linear "growth" as measured by the difference between two standardized test scores. As Ralph Tyler explains the problem,

To many laymen, unfamiliar with the wide range of individual differences in the educational backgrounds of school children, and not knowing the limitations of test norms, the setting of goals seems almost automatic. They state it simply: "Every child should make one year's progress in one year." . . . A test norm represents the average achievement of a representative sample of pupils. Usually half of the sample receives higher scores and half lower scores. A year's progress as indicated by test scores is a figure obtained by subtracting the mean score of pupils in one grade from the mean score of pupils in the grade above. It does not represent any actual measure of the progress made by individual pupils from one year to the next. So the setting of goals is not the simple, nearly automatic, step that laymen have supposed. (51)

While Tyler attributes this attitude to laymen, many educators share it. They accept not only that there is such a unit as "one year's growth per child per year" or "month for month gain" but that these tests yield acceptable measures of it.

Not only performance contract evaluation designs are predicated on this assumption. Many educational programs succeed or fail based on reported test gains. Students are grouped and tracked in schools based on their achievement test scores. But while many areas of education perhaps rely too readily on these test scores, Tyler, R. Stake, R. Lennon, E. G. Joselyn, and others suggest that performance contracts—with their rhetorical emphasis on precise results and their headline publicity—have both aggravated and legitimized this questionable practice.

On the other hand, some educators and some contractors respond that the tests may not be perfect, but they are the best available. If something else had more credibility, it might well be used instead.

If one accepts the appropriateness of using standardized tests for pre-test/post-test measures of growth in performance contracts, the Gary data are rather impressive. As Rand states,

The results of the tests administered in the spring of 1971 were generally favorable, although they left unanswered the question of whether BRL would bring all the students up to norm level in three years. . . . For 546 students in the second to sixth grades, the average gains were 0.72 achievement years in reading and 1.18 in mathematics . . . 41.0 percent of the students made a year's gain in reading and about 66.1 percent made a year's gain in mathematics. (52)

Compared to other contractors in other cities, according to the Rand "box score," Banneker did well. (55)

Yet the Gary data are not as informative as one might wish from an evaluation study. First, a different test was used at Banneker than is used elsewhere in Gary. Second, the test was administered on a different schedule than that regularly followed in Gary. Third, no other comparable population was similarly tested. Therefore one cannot compare Banneker data to other data. Similar problems with test data have occurred in numerous performance contracts.

Of course, for public relations purposes, Gary reported its test results to the press in a manner which maximized their impact, and the Banneker critics dutifully reinterpreted the scores to minimize their impact.

Gary reported scores twice during its first year. A week after Banneker was recommissioned in April, the *Chicago Sun-Times* reported scores from a 20 percent sample of students at Banneker who had been tested in January. According to that report, students were achieving slightly better than month-for-month gains.

They show that on a schoolwide average, students after three months of instruction in reading had advanced slightly more than four months in proficiency. In math they had advanced slightly less than five months in proficiency.

McAndrew said it may be too early to be elated. . . . But he is happy. He believes the results have vindicated him and the school board members for a decision that sparked some of the loudest controversy in recent city history. (54)

TABLE 1

Mean Gains on Standardized Tests[53]

City	LSC	Test Used[a]	Mean Gains	Remarks
Gary	BRL BRL	MAT MAT	1.7/1.7 0.7/1.2	Reading/math, 1st grade Reading/math, grades 2-6
Gilroy	WLC WLC WLC	SAT SAT MAT (Reading)	0.6 0.8 0.6	Reading--for contract payment Math--for contract payment Regular district test
Grand Rapids	Alpha CMES WLC WLC	Various EDS MAT MAT	NR[b] 1.2/1.0[c] 0.7[c] 0.6[c]	Test identification not released by OEO. Three tests used. Reading/math Reading/math Math
Norfolk	LRA LRA	Various[d] Various	0.1 0.5	5th grade 7th and 9th grades
Texarkana	Dorsett Dorsett EDL	ITBS SRA ITBS	NR NR 0.5/0.3	Arkansas Texas Arkansas and Texas, reading/math, grades 6-12

aTest abbreviations: MAT: Metropolitan Achievement Test
 SAT: Stanford Achievement Test
 EDS: Educational Development Series, Scholastic Testing Service
 ITBS: Iowa Test of Basic Skills
 SRA: Science Research Associates Achievement Tests

bNR: data not released.

cMean gains for those students who attended at least 150 days and for whom pre- and post-test scores are available.

dThree tests used at each grade, chosen from SAT, MAT, ITBS, California Achievement, and Stanford Reading Achievement. Means computed only for students who took both a pre-test and a post-test.

In September Banneker achieved nationwide attention following a press conference at which it was reported that during the first year of the project 72.5 percent of 546 children in the program in grades 2 through 6 made average or better than average gains in reading, mathematics, or both. If the calculations had been based upon gains in reading *and* mathematics (as the wording of the contract might have suggested) the percentage would have been a more modest 34.6 percent.

Either way, the Gary scores were "unusually good" especially when compared to other contractors. (55) As Mary Ann Curtis remarked, "It's a miracle that any learning has been able to take place at all, considering the almost constant conflict of one kind or another since Banneker School became Banneker Curriculum Center." (56) As believers in the tests they use, both Gary and BRL anticipate even better scores in years two and three.

In terms of the character of its evaluation, as in almost every other area, Banneker serves as an example of most performance contracts. As with evaluation results from others, one can debate around and through the Gary scores without reaching any firm conslusions.

Although this lack of unequivocal information is frustrating when one hopes to assess success at Banneker or elsewhere, it may well be a cloud with a silver lining. By the very fact that performance contracting has stressed evaluation it may have shown up the generally inadequate quality of educational evaluation in public schools.

Jack Sessions, assistant director of education for the AFL-CIO echoed this conclusion in the January, 1972, *American Teacher,* after listing his frustrations with the Banneker data:

All in all, the published test scores for the Banneker students contain such a mass of inconsistencies, improbabilities, and incongruities that they raise questions stronger, perhaps, than ever before about the value of standardized tests and grade-equivalency scores as dependable measures of educational outputs. The Banneker test scores constitute less a basis for payment than a vindication of the statement by Dr. Henry Dyer of the Educational Testing Service that grade-equivalency scores are "psychological and statistical monstrosities." (57)

Conclusion

Despite fifty other performance contracts during 1970-1971, Banneker swept into the national spotlight and remained there. Nevertheless, Banneker is treated at length in this book not so much for its unique character as for its representativeness, for it exemplifies most other performance contracts in several ways.

Like all others, its essential element is the drama inherent in paying a contractor according to how well students learn. Like most others, Banneker was a contract with a "systems" company for teaching of basic skills (primarily), with a "guarantee" of specified achievement measured by a standardized achievement test. Difficulties with state regulations and teacher organizations inherent within every performance contract all surfaced at Banneker. Like other contracts, Banneker cannot be isolated from local school politics.

Like other contracts during 1970-1971, Banneker began under the glow of praise for Texarkana and the new, ill-understood slogan of "accountability." Like Texarkana and most others, Banneker emerged hastily, incompletely, and imperfectly and had to work out its problems as it proceeded. But also emulating Texarkana, Banneker (and others) maintained a more glittering public image than reality would support.

Internally, Banneker suffered the problems common to most performance contracts: initial naivete, language misunderstanding, squabbles over authority, political and community pressures.

Yet for all its shortcomings, many of those close to Banneker believe it caused some improvements at Banneker, increased some students' learning, increased some teachers' competence, and generally rocked the public school boat with interesting effect. This is substantially the conclusion of the Rand study of Banneker as well, which adds, "Whatever the final outcome of the Banneker program, it should go down in educational history as one of the boldest and most interesting educational experiments in the United States." (58)

Notes

(1) K. S. Goodman, "Promises, Promises," *The Reading Teacher*, 24 (January 1971): 365-7.
(2) G. Saretsky, "Every Kid a Hustler," *Phi Delta Kappan*, 52 (June 1971): 595-596.
(3) G. Saretsky, "Performance Contracting in the Year of the News Release," *ERIC Crier*, (April 1972), pp. 1-3.
(4) P. Schrag, "The Right to Know," *Saturday Review*, 54 (December 18, 1971): 53. ©1971 Saturday Review, Inc.
(5) The exclusive story in the *Chicago Sun-Times* appeared March 15, 1971, reporting the interim test scores from tests given at Banneker. Charles Smith, the union president, and Gordon McAndrew each told me in May, 1971, that no one in Gary knew of the test scores until they had been announced in the *Sun-Times*.
(6) E. Hernandez, "Banneker School a 'Gold Fish Bowl'," *Gary Post-Tribune*, December 20, 1970.
(7) "Banneker at Bay," *Newsweek*, March 15, 1971.
(8) J. A. Mecklenburger and J. A. Wilson, "The Performance Contract in Gary," *Phi Delta Kappan*, 52 (March 1971): 406-410.
(9) G. McAndrew, memo to staff, October 2, 1970.
(10) Hernandez, "Banneker School," citing an interview with Donald Kendrick.
(11) Stated by Gordon McAndrew in an interview with the author and John A. Wilson, at Gary, Indiana, May, 1971.
(12) "School City of Gary Report to State Department of Public Instruction on Banneker Elementary School," February 12, 1971, p. 25-26.
(13) Stated by Otha Porter in an interview with the author and John A. Wilson, at Gary, Indiana, November, 1970.
(14) Hernandez, "Banneker School."
(15) Press release, Hammond Public Schools, July 21, 1971. "The instructors, hired by Learning Foundations, are not licensed teachers. . . . A licensed teacher, however, supervises 9th grade instruction to meet accreditation standards set by the North Central Association for Secondary Schools and Colleges."

(16) Hernandez, "Banneker School."
(17) Stated by Otha Porter in an interview with the author and John A. Wilson, at Gary, Indiana, February, 1972.
(18) N. Postman and C. Weingartner, *The Soft Revolution* (New York: Delacorte, 1971), p. 4.
(19) Stated by Donald Kendrick in an interview with Orest Ochitwa, at Gary, Indiana, October, 1970.
(20) M. P. Berson, "Texarkana and Gary: A Tale of Two Performance Contracts," *Childhood Education,* 47 (March 1971): 339-343, citing an interview with Donald Kendrick at Gary, Indiana, December, 1970.
(21) R. D. James, "How a Corporation Runs an Elementary School and Expects a Profit," *Wall Street Journal,* June 2, 1971, p. 1, citing an interview with Donald Kendrick at Gary, Indiana.
(22) F. Moscove, *The Experiment at Banneker School,* Writers Workshop, Gary, 1971.
(23) Ibid., p. 14-16.
(24) Personal letter written by Francine Moscove to the author, on April 14, 1972.
(25) "MES Guidelines for the 1970's," *American Teacher,* 56 (November 1970): 19.
(26) P. Carpenter and G. H. Hall, *Case Studies in Educational Performance Contracting,* Vol. 1 (Santa Monica: Rand, 1971), p. 38.
(27) D. W. Cray, "What's Happening in Gary?" School Management, 15 (May 1971): 24, citing an interview with George Stern. Excerpted from the May, 1971 issue of *School Management* magazine with permission of the publisher. This article is copyrighted. ©1971 by CCM Professional Magazines, Inc. All rights reserved.
(28) The reader interested in a detailed account of these two conflicts should consult G. R. Hall and M. L. Rapp, *Case Studies in Educational Performance Contracting,* Vol. 4 (Santa Monica: Rand, 1971).
(29) "'Encouraging' Results Reported At Gary," *Education USA,* May 3, 1971, citing Clarence Benford's address to the National Association of Elementary School Principals convention.
(30) E. Hernandez, "Arbitration on Banneker is Continued," *Gary Post-Tribune,* January 21, 1971.
(31) E. Hernandez, "Teachers' Union Won—Or Did It?" *Gary Post-Tribune,* March 1, 1971.
(32) Cray, "What's Happening in Gary?", citing an interview with George Stern.
(33) Minutes, Indiana State Board of Education Meeting, February 18, 1971.
(34) Otha Porter, address made at the Fall Conference of the Indiana School Board Association, French Lick, Indiana, October 14, 1971.
(35) Charles Blaschke, address made at the Fall Conference of the Indiana School Board Association, French Lick, Indiana, October 14, 1971.
(36) Stated by Brian Fitch in an interview with the author and John A. Wilson, in Gary, Indiana, May, 1971.
(37) Ibid.
(38) Hall and Rapp, *Case Studies,* Vol. 4, pp. 29-30.
(39) Ibid., p. 30.
(40) B. Fitch, Memo to Banneker School Curriculum Managers re "Planning for Development, May-September, 1971," May 18, 1971.
(41) Stated by Brian Fitch in an interview with the author and John A. Wilson, in Gary, Indiana, May, 1971.
(42) In contrast, Berson, "Texarkana and Gary," reported her December visit to Banneker. She was ushered into the multipurpose room, then into Kendrick's office, then guided to three classrooms. My own experiences in December and May parallel Berson's and Curtis's.
(43) M. A. Curtis, "Students Playing Games, Coming Up Winners," *Gary Post-Tribune,* June 6, 1971.
(44) Stated by Gordon McAndrew in a telephone interview with the author and John A. Wilson, in Gary, Indiana, August, 1971.
(45) Stated by Ira Judge, physical education teacher at Banneker, in an interview with the author and John A. Wilson, in Gary, Indiana, May 11, 1971.
(46) Fitch, Memo, May 18, 1971.
(47) See especially Mecklenburger and Wilson, "The Performance Contract in Gary"; Cray, "What's Happening in Gary?"; Mecklenburger and Wilson, "Behind the Gary Scores," *Nation's Schools,* 88 (December 1971) 28-29; Hall and Rapp, *Case Studies,* Vol. 4.
(48) L. Feinberg, "Gary's 'Accountability' School—Where Test Scores Mean

Money," *Washington Post,* January 6, 1972, editorial.

(49) Stated by Gordon McAndrew in an interview with the author and John A. Wilson, at Gary, Indiana, December, 1970.

(50) See R. Stake, "Testing Hazards in Performance Contracting," *Phi Delta Kappan,* 52 (June 1971): 583-89; R. Lennon, "To Perform and to Account," *Journal of Research and Development in Education,* 5 (Fall 1971): 3-14; E. G. Joselyn, "Performance Contracting: What It's All About," *American Teacher,* 56 (April 1971): CE 10-11; T. P. Hogan, "Reading Tests and Performance Contracting," mimeo, presented at Indiana Reading Association Conference, January, 1971; R. Tyler, "Testing for Accountability," *Nation's Schools,* 86 (December 1970): 37-39; C. Stokes, "Measuring Gains with Standardized Tests, or, Flies in the Performance Contract Ointment," *NSPI Journal,* 10 (June 1971): 5-6; H. Dyer, "The Role of Evaluation in Accountability," in *Proceedings of the Conference on Educational Accountability,* Educational Testing Service, Princeton, 1971; S. P. Klein, "The Uses and Limitations of Standardized Tests in Meeting the Demands for Accountability," *Evaluation Comment,* 2:1-7; P. Carpenter and G. H. Hall, *Case Studies,* Vol. 1, pp. 15-19.

(51) R. Tyler, "Accountability in Perspective," in L. M. Lessinger and R. W. Tyler, eds., *Accountability in Education* (Worthington, Ohio: Charles A. Jones), 1971.

(52) Hall and Rapp, *Case Studies,* Vol. 4, p. 74.

(53) Carpenter and Hall, *Case Studies,* Vol. 1, p. 14.

(54) D. S. Robinson, "Tests Encourage Backers in Gary School Experiment," *Chicago Sun-Times,* March 15, 1971. Reprinted with permission from the *Chicago Sun-Times.*

(55) Carpenter and Hall, *Case Studies,* Vol. 1, p. 15.

(56) Curtis, *Gary Post-Tribune,* June 6, 1971.

(57) J. A. Sessions, "Performance Contracting Revisited," *American Teacher,* 56 (January 1972): 15.

(58) Hall and Rapp, *Case Studies,* Vol. 4, p. 94.

Part Three

Texarkana

V

The Genesis of Texarkana

Charles Blaschke

"Management," Charles Blaschke said, "is the Achilles heel of public education." (1) Enter Charles Blaschke, change agent. Still under age thirty in 1968, he was very knowledgeable about how other public institutions are managed. A student of institutional change, he received a Harvard degree in public administration with a thesis on "Federal Procurement Policies—A Means to Foster Innovation." He was familiar with the Washington scene, serving one year as acting chief of educational technology for the Office of Economic Opportunity community action program and spending two years of military duty in the office of former Secretary of Defense McNamara. In 1968 he was a Washington-based staff member of the Institute for Politics and Planning (IPP), a management consulting firm.

Between 1969 and 1971 Blaschke became "Mr. Performance Contract." He had coined the term "performance contract-turnkey process" and travelled the conference and convention circuit to promote it. ("Turnkey" was his term, derived from the construction industry, for the time when a project, after being developed by a contractor, is turned over to the funding agent, in this case, the public schools.) He became instrumental in dozens of performance contracts as he formed his own corporation, Education Turnkey Systems, Inc., a management support group specializing in performance contracting and turnkey operations. Especially in 1969 and 1970, Blaschke was the person most reporters consulted when they wished to know about performance contracting. He published widely in educational journals. He began his own newsletter, *Education Turnkey News,* which later became the "Performance Contracting" column in *Nation's Schools* magazine.

But in 1968 and early 1969, Blaschke thought of himself as part of the coterie of "educational technologists" struggling as a profession for recognition and influence. In light of events, it is instructive to recall what Blaschke thought, at that time, needed to be done.

In May, 1969, *Educational Technology,* a trade journal of which Blaschke is a contributing editor, published a special issue which he edited. His theme was the need to create an environment in which educational technology could flourish:

The environment in which the educational technologist attempts to develop and apply the results of his professional endeavor is seldom conducive to the realization of technology's potential.

The lack of effective school management impairs both experimentation and operational use.

The new technology poses inherent conflicts with many political forces, and the technologist, a skilled inventor, is often inadequately trained as an innovator.

Political and managerial innovations are a fundamental prerequisite for the effective application of technology in the learning institutions of the not-so-distant future.

Unfortunately, relatively few federal efforts are being planned to direct attention and resources to the development of political and managerial innovations. Even more disheartening is the malaise and passive reactions to the *very suggestion* that such effort would be worthwhile. (2)

That is, Blaschke believed that politics was intimately related to change; that new styles of management—in effect, different institutions for learning rather than traditional schools—had to be created, politically; that politics at the federal level was needed; and that this effort required technologists trained as innovators. In *Educational Technology* Blaschke sounded a crusading note which he has repeated endlessly since:

For a society so adept in developing advanced technology, we have been grossly inept and negligent in concocting organizations and devising political and managerial innovations to apply technology effectively.

This is true particularly in education. The market for educational technology . . . has to be largely created. . . .

The creation of mechanisms which can—concurrent with the development of technology—direct attention to the political and managerial problems in education is a prerequisite to the effective and creative application of technology in education. (3)

Blaschke edited that magazine concurrently with his efforts to design a performance contract for Texarkana. He makes passing reference to that project in the magazine; obviously, he hoped that performance contracting would be the kind of mechanism he called for—a way to open political doors, a way to create a market, a way to direct attention to problems in education—but he had no way of knowing that Texarkana would be the first of many.

He acknowledged in his introduction to an article on performance contracts in education that there was a need for refining the approach. Blaschke never claimed for performance contracting what other apologists did. He denied it was a panacea. He said it was a limited tool, "a procedure stemming from cost benefit analysis." (4) Its purpose was to "ensure that results are achieved, yet responsible innovation is encouraged." (5)

As for "refinement," throughout the next year Blaschke and others toyed with the terminology, the possible applications, and the possible benefits projected for use of this limited tool. Thus it is misleading to pin down a fixed "Blaschke model" for performance contracts. For Blaschke, performance contracting has remained a concept in transition. Even when in January, 1972, three years later, the Office of Economic Opportunity chose to castigate performance contracting in its report of results of a national experiment, Blaschke issued a press release saying, in effect, that OEO had barely scratched the surface of the concept of performance contracting in the experiment:

Six types of learning systems, rather than performance contracting *per se,* were being tested; performance contracting as a technique of experimentation was successful—where no results occurred, no payment was made.

Over 69 districts in Michigan are under performance contracts ($23 million) with the State Department; in Dade County, Florida, teacher faculties have contracted to double student performance for bonuses of $110 per student. . . . Performance contracting generically has not died; rather, different forms are evolving and expanding. (6)

From Blaschke's perspective, the beauty of performance contracting has been that it focuses on cost—which has political impact—and links cost to learning. Blaschke is fond of saying that all educational decisions are made for political, economic, social, and traditional reasons, and justified afterwards on educational grounds. (7) Thus he views performance contracting as a goal toward fundamental change: he believes improved learning situations will result only when one appeals to the baser reasons by which school decisions are actually made. He says the performance contract process gives school administrators "leverage" for decision-making.

He admits to being a pragmatist, not a philosopher. "I think if you go back to the Industrial Revolution," he said, "you'll find it's always the mechanics that led the revolution and the theoreticians who fifty years later explained why a phenomenon worked." (8)

Gainesville

Blaschke's first attempt to sell performance contracting was for a Gainesville, Georgia, Concentrated Employment Program (CEP) in 1967-1968. Blaschke had the ear of the young director of that program. He persuaded him that an arrangement by which private contractors would "guarantee" to bring trainees to a certain proficiency level in the least amount of time, for the least cost, would cost approximately one-third of traditional programs. According to Blaschke, it became evident that federal, regional, and state officials "would not support the program because of its implications and its radical break with tradition." (9) A further attempt to link the program to dropout prevention in the Gainesville schools also received a cold shoulder. During the controversy, the CEP director resigned.

Although the bureaucracy opposed the concept, there had been some support from White House and HEW officials, confirming in Blaschke's mind that "inadequate managerial skills of local government agencies" are barriers to innovation. "It taught those of us developing the concept that the site at which the concept would be next applied would have to have a climate more favorable to innovation than the first." (10)

Blaschke Discovers Texarkana

Blaschke knew nothing of Texarkana until a friend of a friend, who knew of his interest in performance contracts, told him of the many problems demanding solution in the Texarkana schools. Vacationing with family in Texas, he received a call from Joe Hart of the University of Arkansas who knew Blaschke through association with the Institute for Politics and Planning. Hart had perceived that Blaschke's concept of performance contracting might be welcomed in Texarkana which was currently in the throes of conflict occasioned by school integration.

At Hart's suggestion, Blaschke came to Texarkana to meet Tom McRae, Model Cities Director there, whom Blaschke describes as "a young but managerially competent and politically sensitive former Peace Corps and poverty warrior." (11)

McRae was pleased with Blaschke's ideas and hastily arranged a meeting with the three Texarkana school district superintendents. Within a week, to meet a deadline in Washington, the three districts, with Blaschke and Hart serving as consultants, had jointly requested a planning grant under the newly funded dropout prevention amendment, Title VIII of the Elementary and Secondary Education Act.

As Blaschke said later, "The climate for innovation in Texarkana appeared conducive to the application of performance contracting not only in terms of educational merit, but also in terms of the political and social criteria of acceptance." (12) This was not Gainesville. Dropout rates were very high in Texarkana schools, especially in the Texarkana, Arkansas' black high school, where rates rose as high as 17 percent annually. School achievement was correspondingly low. It was predicted that merging white and black high school populations, who score far apart on standardized achievement tests, would increase the number of dropouts merely by academic frustration and embarrassment of black students. On the other hand, whites feared desegregation because it might mean lowering of school quality. Model Cities, with a heavy black constituency in Texarkana, acted as a change agent under McRae's leadership, and he recognized a program around which to rally. Finally, according to Blaschke,

Several board members . . . felt that existing teacher certification, class size, and other state and local regulations which created inefficiency, could be demonstrated (by this program) to be the shibboleths that they were and that new legislation could be enacted if the program were successful. (13)

Under Blaschke's leadership, the districts proposed a plan which complemented the Model Cities five-year Action Plan. They proposed a five-year multifaceted dropout prevention program, the academic component for the first year of which was to be an Accelerated Learning Achievement Center for secondary school students, contracted with a private corporation on a performance contract basis. Blaschke depicted performance contracting as a low cost, low risk procedure for efficient innovation; it would first scour the marketplace for the best program for Texarkana, and deliver it at the lowest possible price.

Blaschke proposed to school officials there that instead of trying to solve their problem unassisted, they specify the educational accomplishment they wanted to produce; let him write a proposal for federal funds . . . send out a request for proposals and invite firms in the education business to submit their bids. . . . Blaschke pointed out that if the program should fail, the contractor would bear the burden, and if it worked, as he expected it would, the schools could thus help many children who, in effect, had reluctantly been given up for lost. He added that if the firm were required to train local personnel in the operation of the program, the schools could easily absorb it into their regular curriculum when the contract expired; and that if the federal grant would pay for preliminary planning and management support, the whole project would require a bare minimum of extra work by the school system itself.

How could they lose? (14)

To summarize, in Leon Lessinger's words, Blaschke, "a talented and persuasive young consultant, sold the idea." (15)

Between the preliminary proposal in December for a planning grant and the formal proposal in May for a five-year dropout prevention program, Blaschke conducted an informal version of what later was called "needs assessment."

"Needs assessment" is a systematic attempt to specify what educational accomplishments are needed, and to rank their priority by seeking all appropriate counsel and advice. Seeking of counsel and advice serves two purposes: it may improve the quality of a subsequent educational program and perhaps more important, it tests the political environment in which a program must sink or swim. As Blaschke stated in his formal proposal to USOE,

To plan an operational program which is experimental and also is conducted in a political and social environment, one necessarily has to put politics into planning. (16)

According to information in the proposal, Blaschke had begun in January to describe possible approaches and to seek suggestions and support from the Texarkana Chamber of Commerce, several churches, both city halls, both police chiefs, Texas and Arkansas education officials, USOE officials, state and national congressmen, private corporations, other schools, education journals, local teachers and teacher organizations, youth organizations, and civic clubs. In addition, he formed a working advisory group of fifteen representative Texarkana school officials.

Texarkana Comes to Washington

After Blaschke's failure to implement performance contracting in Gainesville, a new political administration came to Washington. Leon Lessinger, Associate Commissioner of Education in the U. S. Office of Education, had responsibility for the Elementary and Secondary Education Act. In that position, he was keenly aware that Congress and the president, although not undisposed to education spending, increasingly insisted on results for federal money expended.

One example of this new Washington sensibility was Senator George Murphy's proposal, which became law in 1968, to create demonstration projects for preventing school dropouts among school districts with large percentages of poor children. He insisted on innovative methods and objective annual measurement. This program, modestly budgeted at $5 million, fell to Lessinger in USOE; it included money for planning grants and was the amendment to Title VIII under which the Texarkana project fell.

While Lessinger modestly disowns the label given him as "father" of the concept of "accountability," it was during his tenure that "in the period 1968-1969, federal guidelines for the expenditure of discretionary funds in a portion of the Elementary and Secondary Education Act mandated accountability provisions. The rest is history." (17)

Accountability has been a word with a shifting collection of meanings, changing from proponent to proponent and over time. But at that time, before it mushroomed into a slogan and Lessinger became its chief proponent, the focus of accountability was effective expenditure of federal funds.

According to Lessinger, testifying before a House subcommittee on President Nixon's first budget, those accountability procedures of

ESEA included a) goal setting at the local level, b) evaluation in terms of the goals set, c) technical assistance, and d) independent educational accomplishment audits. These obviously are management concepts.

Lessinger described technical assistance as

The use of resources outside the local education agency in planning, developing, operating, evaluating, auditing and disseminating educational programs. There are numerous sources for this assistance. Particularly helpful to applicants will be business and industry which can supply new emphasis on improved management capabilities. (18)

Of the term accountability, as it was being applied to dropout prevention programs, Lessinger told the committee:

Basically, accountability means that the grantee will be held responsible at any time during the project for accomplishing the objectives of the project which the grantee himself proposed. . . . There will be a benchmark against which to measure performance.

You will be interested as the months go by in those project centers all over the country which will be using this notion of accountability. They will focus on the results that have been achieved. (19)

It is no accident that this testimony, given May 6th, described the Texarkana project and its implications, although Lessinger did not mention Texarkana by name. As the project began the next fall, he spearheaded a national effort to popularize the term "accountability" in which he constantly pointed to Texarkana as the best example. While Blaschke toured the country promoting performance contracting, Lessinger, who could reach larger audiences, stressed accountability and a related term, "educational engineering." During that year he published a book, *Every Kid a Winner—Accountability in Education.* Although the book discussed the concept of accountability and its utility, most of its space was devoted to the Texarkana project. Lessinger also published several widely quoted articles in education periodicals which stressed accountability as seen in Texarkana. President Nixon's March 3rd, 1970, educational policy address, which helped spark the 1970-1971 rash of performance contracts, borrowed heavily from Lessinger's ideas, including the new concept: *accountability.*

Whatever political maneuvering occurred in Washington over the Texarkana proposal has never been revealed in detail, but one can piece together hints of it.

Texarkana's planning grant proposal, which Blaschke wrote, quickly reached Lessinger's desk after it was submitted in December. Obviously, it meshed with his thinking and direction. Lessinger reports that the proposal had his support (20) and Blaschke reports that

The project probably would not have been funded had it not been for "encouragement" from both Associate Commissioner Leon Lessinger and

Arkansas and Texas congressmen, senators, and high-level state officials. (21)

The final Texarkana proposal was submitted to the U. S. Office of Education May 3, 1969, three days before Lessinger's testimony quoted earlier. Two weeks prior to that, Lessinger had asked Blaschke to brief him and his staff on the Texarkana project and its implications. During that meeting, Blaschke says, "It became apparent that the project would have high level support although many bureaucratic and other barriers would have to be overcome within USOE." (22) It was scarcely a month later that word came to Arkansas and Texas Congressmen that a grant had been awarded.

But a political skirmish centered on whether Texarkana, Texas, would be included. A referendum there had endorsed a "Freedom of Choice" plan over HEW objections, and on the basis that the city did not meet HEW guidelines its involvement in the dropout prevention project was "deferred." The project budget was cut, ostensibly because of this, to $250,000 from the $750,000 originally proposed. A second referendum in Texarkana offered voters the choice of the dropout prevention program versus Freedom of Choice; 71 percent favored the Federal program. However, by that time, Texarkana, Texas, was too late to reapply for funds. Blaschke said this was the excuse, not the cause, of the budget cut:

At a meeting between representatives of the Texarkana planning group and Office of Education officials, it became apparent that the performance contract approach had high-level support within the Office of Education, as well as the Department of Health, Education and Welfare, but was meeting with resistance at lower levels in those bureaucracies. The reasons for resistance included ideological opposition, doubts whether the approach would work, many fears that the educational community would be bitter toward any agency which funded such a project. The funding of any proposal submitted to the Office of Education is highly dependent upon favorable reviews from "panels of experts" who are usually housed in universities, or other such groups who bear a large responsibility for the present status of education. It was not too surprising to learn that the review panel had put the Texarkana proposal at a relatively low rating among the twenty dropout prevention proposals eventually funded.

One suspects an additional reason for opposition was that the approach caused administrative problems for the Office of Education. For example, because the contractor had not been selected at that time, the planners could not list in the proposal the specific equipment to be purchased. Administrators frowned upon any projects which used subcontractors for a majority of the services. And, because a performance contract had never been written, the legal and contracts officers were concerned about its legality. (23)

From its inception, those who supported the Texarkana project outside of Texarkana had much larger visions than merely improving the school system. Texarkana was perceived by Blaschke, Lessinger, and others as the beginning of substantive changes in American education. Said Lessinger: "The public school system is being held accountable for results. Accountability is the coming sine qua non for education in the 1970s." He added, "Performance contracting is *one* process for which accountability is the product." (24)

Under the title, "The Coming Revolution in American Education," Congressman Roman Pucinski, Chairman of the House Subcommittee on General Education, entered a description of the Texarkana project into the *Congressional Record* in August. He claimed that guaranteed performance contracting is

a concept in American education which in my judgment offers great promise of major breakthroughs in raising achievement skills for our nation's young people. . . . If it succeeds in Texarkana, it is a concept that we will want to employ throughout the country. (25)

In an article appearing in December, 1969, Lessinger wrote, "Such a concept may have far-reaching implications toward efficiency of education in years to come." (26) Both Congressman Pucinski and Senator George Murphy had this article written into the *Congressional Record.*

Notes

(1) Stated by Charles Blaschke in an interview with the author, in Washington, D. C., April, 1971.
(2) C. Blaschke, "Introduction," *Educational Technology*, 6 (May 1970): 10.
(3) C. Blaschke, "Computers in Education: Interesting, But How Relevant?" *Educational Technology*, 6 (May 1969): 24, 29.
(4) C. Blaschke, "Introduction," op. cit.
(5) C. Blaschke, P. Briggs, and R. Martin, "The Performance Contract-Turnkey Approach to Urban School System Reform," *Educational Technology*, 9 (September 1970): 45.
(6) C. Blaschke, "The OEO Project Results," press release, February 1, 1972.
(7) In *Education Turnkey News*, 1 (April 1970): 1, Blaschke said, "Innovative educational programs are usually sold and accepted on the basis of political, social, and economic merits and justified after the fact on the basis of educational factors."
(8) Stated by Charles Blaschke in a question and answer session, National School Boards Association conference on performance contracting, Chicago, Illinois, February 5, 1971.
(9) Charles Blaschke, "Performance Contracting: Who Profits Most?" Quotations are from an unedited manuscript, much of which was subsequently published. See Charles Blaschke, *Performance Contracting: Who Profits Most?* (Bloomington, Indiana: Phi Delta Kappa Educational Foundation, 1972).
(10) Blaschke, "Performance Contracting: Who Profits Most?"
(11) Ibid.
(12) Ibid.
(13) Ibid.
(14) Leon Lessinger, *Every Kid a Winner—Accountability in Education* (New York: Simon and Schuster, 1970), pp. 93-94.
(15) Ibid., p. 91.
(16) C. Blaschke, *Project Application to the U. S. Office of Education,* Part III, "Program Planning," May 3, 1969.
(17) L. Lessinger, "A Historical Note on Accountability in Education," *Journal of Research and Development in Education* (Atlanta, Ga.: University of Georgia, College of Education, Fall 1971), 5, p. 15.
(18) L. Lessinger, "Hearings before a Subcommittee of the Committee on Appropriations, House of Representatives," 91st Congress, May 6, 1969; excerpted in Lessinger, "Historical Note."

(19) Ibid.
(20) Lessinger, *Every Kid a Winner,* p. 94.
(21) Blaschke, "Performance Contracting: Who Profits Most?".
(22) Ibid.
(23) Education Turnkey Systems, *Performance Contracting in Education,* Research Press, Champaign, Illinois, 1970, p. 9.
(24) L. Lessinger, "Engineering Accountability for Results in Public Education," *Phi Delta Kappan,* 51 (December 1970): 217.
(25) Hon. Roman C. Pucinski, "The Coming Revolution in American Education," *Congressional Record,* 91st Congress: E7021, August 13, 1969.
(26) L. Lessinger, "After Texarkana, What?" *Nation's Schools,* 84 (December 1969): 38.

VI

Implementation
of the Texarkana Project

Selecting the Contractor

In one major procedural way, Texarkana differed substantially from the Banneker project. Whereas Banneker began with an informal agreement between a school district and a corporation, Texarkana proceeded from "needs assessment" through proposals and planning to competitive bidding to select a contractor. During 1970-1971, these two approaches were differentiated by several writers (1) as "competitive bidding" and "sole source" models of performance contracting. There were more sole source contracts 1969-1971 than competitive contracts.

With Blaschke spearheading the Texarkana effort, it is no surprise that performance contracting was employed in Texarkana as a device to choose among educational technology companies. Blaschke never discussed the sole source possibility, nor did he mention that performance contracts would be an alternative device for contracting with local teachers or with any other organization. Not until 1971 did Blaschke give attention to these permutations of his ideas.

Of course, Blaschke was dealing from strength. He had four years of experience working with educational technology companies, which gave him the contacts and the leverage to excite some educational "systems" companies about this Texarkana opportunity. James Gillis, for example, who wrote the performance contract article for Blaschke's 1969 special *Educational Technology* issue, as president of Quality Educational Development (QED) was among the bidders for the Texarkana contract.

To education companies, Texarkana represented a way to reach the public school market, as Blaschke had written in *Educational Technology*. The growing high-level government interest in performance contracting and "accountability" promised that success in Texarkana would open much larger markets afterward.

Thus in retrospect it comes as no surprise that of the 113 corporations Blaschke identified as potential bidders to whom he sent the Texarkana RFP (request for proposals), over forty expressed sufficient interest to attend a bidders' conference in Texarkana, including such giants as IBM, RCA, and McGraw-Hill. Eventually several companies submitted the complex proposal document required by the RFP. (Varying reports say as few as nine to as many as seventeen companies submitted proposals.) These included Behavioral Research Laboratories (BRL), Learning Foundations, Plan Education Centers, QED, Educational Development Laboratory (a division of McGraw-Hill), Macmillan Educational Services, and RCA Service Company—all of whom subsequently held performance contracts elsewhere.

Texarkana selected Dorsett Educational Systems, a manufacturer of teaching machines, from Norman, Oklahoma. Dorsett proposed a combination of audio-visual equipment and programmed teaching materials, relying heavily on the AVTM-86 teaching machine Dorsett had developed. It was said that the machine has fifty transistors and a computer-style shift register, that it took thirteen years to develop at a cost to Dorsett of $2 million, and that it was quite a spectacular device priced inexpensively at $200 per machine. (2) It synchronizes film presentation and sound recordings and responds by voice to students' correct and incorrect answers . Texarkana would be the first major demonstration of this machine.

Dorsett's proposal relied heavily on Job Corps and other self-paced instructional materials which would need to be adapted to the Dorsett machine. In addition, Dorsett proposed to develop a large number of instructional modules during the year, at the company's expense.

Dorsett proposed Rapid Learning Centers—remodelled classrooms intended to change the image of schooling. They would be carpeted and air-conditioned with comfortable furniture, soft lighting, and an area for relaxation. In addition, Dorsett intended to use short-term and long-term rewards to students, ranging from green stamps for a student finishing a learning module to a television set for the student with greatest tested achievement. He also intended to offer stock options to teachers, who would be in his employ.

Dorsett "guaranteed" at least one year's growth per student for each eighty hours of instruction, for $80. Dorsett would receive more money if the student achieved more gain, or achieved the one year's gain in less time. If the student failed to achieve one year's gain, Dorsett would not be paid.

Although the procedures for selecting a contractor in Gary and in Texarkana differed, one should note that the decision to enter a performance contract was sold in a similar fashion—that is, school officials and an interested party (George Stern in Gary, Blaschke in

Texarkana) held an informal discussion in which they concluded that such an arrangement was of mutual interest.

But because the money for Texarkana was to come from the Federal government, the complex formal process of contracting with Blaschke proposed to Texarkana seemed more appropriate there than it did to school officials in Gary, who dismissed it. Gary money was local, to come chiefly from the district's usual resources of local and state tax monies. (3) And the Gary decision merely required the approval of the school board.

Many school personnel, in cities which chose sole source performance contracts in 1970, have told me they think the RFP-competitive bidding procedure is unnecessary unless a funding agency requires it. A typical view is that the school knows what it wants and that a company knows what it can sell.

A Development Project

Banneker and Texarkana differ over many particulars, such as the size of the program, length, number of students, teaching materials, and source of funding. But most elements of each project find parallel in the other.

As with BRL at Banneker, the companies that bid in Texarkana (which included BRL) were not offering ready-made programs which they were able to use in the Texarkana setting. After all, this was their first entry into a new market; there had been little interest among schools in purchasing complete instructional systems. In order to respond to the RFP, each company had been compelled to speculate on how it might quickly implement an instructional system in Texarkana; each company was aware it would need to develop its program there. That is, these companies were not offering finished wares; they were selling ideas, techniques, procedures, and a "systems" way of thinking that the company *hoped* would succeed. (If Gary officials had understood this about the Texarkana experience, they might have had more realistic expectations for the BRL proposal. If OEO officials had understood this, they might have designed their 1970-1971 national experiment differently.)

The nationwide publicity surrounding the idea of a "guarantee" submerged this aspect of the Texarkana project. Most articles about the program, once it was underway, did not mention that Dorsett was busy writing materials as the project continued; no one mentioned the confusion of roles among the participants, which later was revealed in the evaluator's report; and no one stressed the lengthy negotiations over the Texarkana contract itself as the parties jockeyed with one another to define what each might do—the contract was not signed until well after the program started.

In short, Texarkana, like Banneker, was a development project; Dorsett was developing an instructional system, Texarkana was developing a drop-out prevention program. The company and the school district were sharing the financial risk. Despite accusations that companies would be making profit on children, the Texarkana project cost Dorsett twice what the firm might receive on the contract. (4)

But most outsiders did not perceive the developmental nature of the Rapid Learning Centers, nor were they meant to. Those visitors who dropped into Texarkana during the project, unless they asked probing questions, would not have seen any evidence. The rhetoric of the proposals, the contract with Dorsett, as well as the publicity, all gave the impression of certainty, not improvisation.

Emphasis on Cost

As at Banneker, the Texarkana project placed a heavy emphasis on cost, for similar reasons of politics and finances. When Texarkana chose one among its several bidders, the major criterion was cost. This reflects Blaschke's thinking that the competitive bidding aspect of performance contracts imitates the marketplace and enables a school board to purchase services on the basis of cost-effectiveness. It also reflects the realities of Texarkana's school finances and the Federal "accountability" emphasis. Bucky Ussery, director of instruction for Texarkana schools, said the school district looked ahead to the days when it would take over ("turnkey," in Blaschke's terminology) the contractor's program:

We were not looking for something that's successful and costly. We wanted something that would be successful and could fit into Texarkana's school budget. (5)

In Gary superintendent Gordon McAndrew had likewise instructed BRL that the project should "cost no more" than an average Gary school.

In both cases, when BRL and Dorsett spent beyond the value of their contract it was a bonus to the school district. Texarkana and Banneker both can be understood as loss leaders aimed at the education market, with Gary and Texarkana the fortunate bargain hunters. Performance contracts between schools and private corporations can be a mutually beneficial umbrella under which to develop new products—in these cases, "systems" of instruction.

As Brian Fitch said in Gary, performance contracts offer "a basis for negotiations between independent systems developers and school people." Similarly, Ruth Hayre, superintendent of District 4 in Philadelphia, saw the Philadelphia contract with BRL as "the first time in the history of Philadelphia Schools, during which millions of dollars had been spent on reading materials with various and sundry publishers, . . . that any publisher indicated willingness to be accountable and to share partnership with the school staff. . . ." (6)

Linguistic and Role Confusion

Because day-to-day information is sketchy from Texarkana, it is difficult to resurrect many details of the workings of the project. Nevertheless, what evidence there is points to similar confusions of language and role as occurred at Banneker. Rand adds that these confusions occurred in most performance contracts it studied. (7)

Texarkana may have been plagued by too many cooks. Blaschke came to Texarkana to promote an idea. He convinced Tom McRae of Model Cities in Texarkana, who in turn convinced the three school superintendents who agreed to let Blaschke create a planning grant proposal to USOE. That involved Lessinger, his staff, and other USOE and HEW officials. Then Blaschke sought advice and commitment from dozens of other people in and out of Texarkana. Once the planning grant was approved, Blaschke and Joe Hart returned as agents of the Institute for Politics and Planning (IPP). In Washington, cross fertilization kept Blaschke in close contact with Lessinger and his staff, some of whom later joined Blaschke's staff when he formed Education Turnkey Systems.

There was a role for the contractor, Dorsett, whose vice-president, Charles J. Donnelly, became Resident Director. He was assisted by a number of "instructional consultants." Texarkana appointed Martin J. Filagamo as its Project Director. As in Gary, the respective roles of company and school directors were not defined. The teachers and aides in the learning centers were Dorsett employees, yet they worked within the personnel and the constraints of the public schools. The relationships of school superintendents, Loyd Dorsett, Donnelly, Filagamo, their assistants, and staff were left to work out in practice.

Add the ill-defined tasks of the "management support group" (MSG) who provided guidance and assistance as needed. Blaschke filled the role, first as an agent of IPP subservient to the Texarkana superintendents, later as president of Education Turnkey Systems subservient to Filagamo. As he grew as a national celebrity he had less and less input to the project itself.

There was a role for evaluation—sometimes labelled "internal" and sometimes "independent." In this role, Texarkana hired the Arkansas Region VIII Education Service Center in Magnolia, Arkansas. Its role was never precise, neither as to the information to be collected, the form to report it in, to whom to report it, or when. The evaluation function evolved, as sometimes Blaschke and sometimes the "independent educational auditor" found themselves performing the same tasks. EPIC Diversified Systems, of Tucson, Arizona, was to oversee and certify the evaluation. Although it was supposed to begin in December, its contract was not signed until March. The evaluation function became more snarled when scandal over testing broke in May; not only did the evaluator investigate and re-investigate, but so did Blaschke, EPIC, the school board, and

USOE; the latter two hired Educational Testing Service as an additional consultant on the problem.

During the project, there grew between Lessinger and Blaschke a rough model of the "performance contract" process; yet the two never seemed to agree upon emphasis or terminology. What Blaschke called the "performance contract-turnkey process, a catalyst for school system reform" Lessinger called "educational engineering for accountability." The resulting impermanence of the terminology within the project itself can be surmised. To read what Lessinger, Blaschke, Filagamo, Donnelly, Dorsett, Superintendent Trice, the evaluator and auditor wrote about such key terms as "performance contract," "accountability," "audit," and "turnkey" confirms the impression that the many parties to the project must have sometimes found it difficult to converse.

In sum, the Texarkana project contained many people in many imprecisely defined roles doing something none of them had done before (nor anyone else) using language new to them all. In such a situation, Peter Briggs (first of Lessinger's, then Blaschke's staff) once told me, the systems approach "boils down to working by the seat of one's pants." (8) Items from the internal evaluator's report hint at the confusion that sometimes existed behind the headlines:

The contract with Dorsett Company was not finalized until sometime after the project was in operation and did not require the company to achieve all goals and objectives outlined in the Dorsett proposal.

The roles of the project director, resident director, internal evaluator, management support, and external auditor were not outlined sufficiently to determine who was responsible for what.

There needed to be more correlation between the school district's Title VII program and those programs sponsored by Model Cities. It was not always clear which programs and which students should be included in the evaluation.

A number of students were placed in the rapid learning center program who did not fulfill the criteria of the target population.

Students might be in the program several days or weeks when they should have been out of the program. On one occasion several students were reported as exited from the program but were not.

Dorsett was not satisfied with the tests. . . . This caused a number of problems with no one knowing who was to make a final decision.

From conversations and contact between management support and internal evaluator, there appeared to be overlapping functions, and both were seeking some of the same information.

It was difficult to get an adequate description of the rapid learning center instructional program because many of Dorsett's plans and materials were in the developmental stage. . . .

A number of problems arose during the operation of the project. Some of the problems were results of lack of planning; others were due to lack of guidelines; some were due to unclear understanding of roles and functions; some were due to slow negotiations in the contract; some were due to a reduction in funds; and others were unanticipated problems that occur when any new developmental program is initiated. (9)

Pedagogy and Standardized Testing

As noted earlier, the first question raised when people hear that contractors will be paid according to test scores is, "What will constrain the contractor from teaching the test answers?"

In the early drafts of the contract with Dorsett, several provisions addressed this problem: Dorsett would post a performance bond; he would be assigned a controlled vocabulary of 4000 words any of which he could teach; a retention test, six months after the program, would affect final payment to the contractor. During negotiations which followed the reduction of funding from $750,000 to $250,000, all these clauses were struck. Nor was there ever a specific contract provision prohibiting teaching of test items.

Texarkana and Dorsett agreed in their contract upon specific tests with which to measure student performance. Further, it was understood that Dorsett would analyze the tests to determine what vocabulary and skills the tests sample. Then, as Dorsett adapted and developed teaching materials to the teaching machine he would be certain to teach those vocabulary and skills. Thus, the test was the objective, in the contractor's eyes. In effect, since neither Dorsett nor Texarkana had a set of objectives for mathematics or reading, they agreed to abide by the objectives inherent in the tests. The tests created the curriculum.

Banneker differed from Texarkana in this regard. The curriculum was selected first; BRL materials already had objectives built in which became the objectives for Banneker School. The "textbook" created the curriculum. At Banneker the outside evaluator selected the test on other criteria than instructional objectives, choosing the Metropolitan Achievement Test because

it was completely revised and renormed, after approximately ten years of study and effort, and will be available for the first time in school year 1970-1971. During the revision, special efforts were made to eliminate ethnic irrelevance and cultural unsuitability which made earlier standardized tests inappropriate for the measurement of the achievement of the inner city child. (10)

In selecting the test this way, BRL submitted itself to the opposite danger from that inherent in Dorsett's procedure: students might learn according to instructional objectives but the test might not reveal this. Other performance contractors may have suffered financial loss this way.

For six months of the Dorsett project, testing was not at issue. Students entering the learning center took a standardized achievement test. Several hours of instruction later, they took another. Students who achieved at least one year's gain in reading and mathematics—that is, enough for the contractor to receive payment—were returned to regular classes and replaced by another student.

Everyone skirted the question whether this testing procedure was valid, reliable, or sufficiently precise to yield measures of student achievement.

In December Dorsett chose 27 students and administered standardized tests to each. Although the results were "for project management purposes only," they were published outside Texarkana, since they suited the purposes of performance contract advocates.

The average grade level increase in reading skills of all those properly assigned students who were tested with alternate forms of the same test instrument (for pre- and post-testing) was 2.01 grade levels in reading and 1.09 levels in mathematics. Assuming that 28 hours were spent on reading study and 20 hours were spent on mathematics, this implies one grade level increase per 14 hours in reading and per 18 hours in mathematics. (11)

In February, 51 students, after 89 total hours of instruction, were achieving .99 grade level increases in mathematics, 1.50 in reading. In March, 45 students, after a total of 120 hours of instruction, were achieving 2.2 grade level increases in reading and 1.4 in math. (12)

Senator George Murphy read the February test scores into the *Congressional Record,* February 28th, 1970. The widely circulated newsletter *Education USA* released the scores also. Martin J. Filagamo, Texarkana's Project Director, reported the March test scores in *Today's Education* for May, 1970, reaching over 1,000,000 readers. Blaschke, Lessinger, and others also conveyed them by word of mouth. No wonder Gordon McAndrew, in Gary, paid attention to performance contracting.

In reports of test scores, the impression was left in many minds that all students tested had been chosen randomly from the student population, as was done the next year in Gary for its mid-year sample. This, however, was not the case.

When exit tests were scheduled, Dorsett Company recommended the students to take such tests. . . . Students in rapid learning centers could take the exit test more than once. In addition, they might be given practice tests by Dorsett prior to exit tests. (13)

The Texarkana project sought to bring a student up to grade level as quickly as possible and return him to the regular operating classroom. . . . Thus, the students who seemed to be achieving the best were the first to be tested. The results were understandably dramatic but did not really furnish a sample of what was going on in the overall project. (14)

From October to May 351 students attended the Rapid Learning Centers. The number tested in December, February, and March—27, 51, and 45 respectively—constitutes only 123 students; since the scores reported were averages, some may not have scored sufficiently. In effect, the scores reported nationwide which found school systems "going stark, raving Texarkana" (15) were those of the 100 or so students who did best in the program. They did not represent the total student population.

Regardless, in May of 1970, the world could not have seemed rosier for Loyd Dorsett, Lessinger, Blaschke, et al. Many big cities were beginning to announce that they too would have performance contracts the next year—Gary, Dallas, Philadelphia, and more.

But a student in one of the Rapid Learning Centers told Filagamo, as he toured testing sites during May, that he had previously seen an item on the achievement test he was taking. Indeed he had. Subsequent investigation yielded prima facie evidence that students had been studying test items.

The story broke piece by piece and became worse with each report; but with several investigations and counterclaims, even now the facts are not clear and short of a court case may never be. (16) It was alleged that students had been required to study certain specific materials before taking tests. Dorsett claimed that the final payment tests were contaminated only marginally while the evaluators claimed the contamination was irrevocable. In the face of such claims, scandal swept the Texarkana project.

"Teaching the test" was headlines. It became the ignominious sin that critics needed to shatter performance contracting. The AFT's *American Teacher* particularly grasped the political paydirt in this story and month after month used it to condemn the hucksters, the accountants, and the educational-industrial complex.

As *Educational Researcher* politely reported,

The reports of irregularities . . . have sent a wave of unease through the ranks of schoolmen, researchers, and contractors who for a variety of reasons see great potential in performance contracting as a way to make the schools more accountable to the public. It will also serve to confirm what critics believe to be the most serious weakness of such a system, namely the temptation to concentrate on tests and to take questionable shortcuts. (17)

Nearly two years later, news stories about performance contracting continue to recall the "teaching the test" scandal. (18)

The News of Texarkana

Two kinds of information about Texarkana were available during most of the 1969-1970 project:

First, there were statements issued by the school district personnel, Blaschke, Lessinger, Dorsett, Congressman Pucinski, and Senator Murphy and others who wished to promote performance contracting, educational technology, and "accountability." This was by far the most frequent kind of information. It was general, biased, and evangelical, albeit exciting. Reports of test scores were the epitome of this kind of information.

Second, there were reports of those who visited Texarkana. These tended to be school superintendents or their representatives, state and federal officials, education companies and their friends, and possible clients of Blaschke and Dorsett. The overwhelming number of visitors were either curious or friendly to the project. The next year Banneker would draw thousands of visitors whereas Texarkana drew 800; from the beginning Banneker would draw dozens of reporters and several television film crews, whereas Texarkana drew few reporters until late in the year. Banneker would be the center of controversy from its inception—partly due to the Texarkana scandal—and would draw many hostile visitors who conveyed their impressions in print. Texarkana caused no hostility until it ended; therefore news coverage of Texarkana was scattered and rather perfunctory. The two major exceptions either had small circulation or were published as the project ended. (19)

Just as with Banneker but moreso, therefore, most people knew almost nothing about the inner workings of the Texarkana project except what its partisans chose to reveal. It is ironic that in Texarkana, the birthplace of "accountability," public relations overwhelmed accounts.

Conclusion

It may be true that management is the Achilles heel of public education, but the Achilles heel of management is evaluation. To this Blaschke had been blinded, as he designed Texarkana, by his concern for cost-effectiveness; its simple dollars-over-test-score appeal masked the inherent complexity of evaluation. In designing Texarkana, he desired the project to demonstrate new sophistication in school management and instruction. Lessinger, too, favored the project for this reason. At least in design (if not always in execution), it did. Yet they chose to mask complexity by one simplistic measure.

It was a pragmatic choice, a politic choice, for in the public eye standardized achievement test results have great credibility. Moreover, risking an important enterprise on a single measure has dramatic flair and calls attention to itself. But the whole of an exciting enterprise was jeopardized by the choice.

Most contracts in 1970-1971 attempted to buttress the tests but maintained them as a measure of effectiveness. Blaschke and Lessinger have each modified their thinking since. Blaschke has included other measures in contracts he designed, while Lessinger has expanded his "accountability" emphasis to include many measures of many kinds of objectives. (20) Blaschke's newest emphasis is cost; he has left determination of effectiveness to others. (21)

In light of Texarkana, one might expect several other contracts to have tripped over the testing/evaluation hurdle. Many did.

Notes

(1) For example, see J. Stenner and M. H. Kean, "Four Approaches to Education Performance Contracting," *Educational Leadership* 28 (April 1971): 721-25.

(2) S. M. Elam, "The Age of Accountability Dawns in Texarkana," *Phi Delta Kappan*, 50 (June 1970): 512.

(3) In an interview with the author, Ivanhoe Donaldson, of the Cummins Foundation, stated that a $100,000 annual grant to the Gary Schools for the purpose of innovation had been assigned to Banneker School in 1970-1971.

(4) D. C. Andrew and L. H. Roberts, *Final Evaluation Report on the Texarkana Dropout Prevention Program*, Region VIII Education Service Center, Magnolia, Arkansas, July 20, 1970, p. 49, citing a letter from Loyd Dorsett to Ed Trice, May 28, 1970.

(5) John Morton, "Private Company Teaches Students on Cash Contract," *National Observer*, December 12, 1969, page 11, citing an inverview with Bucky Ussery, in Texarkana, Arkansas. Reprinted with permission from *The National Observer*, Copyright, 1969, Dow Jones and Co., Inc.

(6) Ruth W. Hayre, press release, Philadelphia Public Schools, August 23, 1971.

(7) P. Carpenter, A. W. Chalfant, and G. R. Hall, *Case Studies in Educational Performance Contracting*, Volume 3, *Texarkana, Arkansas and Liberty Eylau, Texas*, (Santa Monica: Rand, 1971), p. 28.

(8) Stated by Peter Briggs in an interview with the author in Washington, D. C., May, 1971.

(9) Andrew and Roberts, Final Evaluation Report, p. 33-38.

(10) Center for Urban Redevelopment and Education, "Proposal for the Evaluation of the Contracted Curriculum Center, Gary, Indiana," August, 1970, p. 7.

(11) Education Turnkey Systems, *Performance Contracting in Education* (Champaign, Illinois: Research Press, 1970), p. 12.

(12) *Education Turnkey News* 1 (April 1970): 6.

(13) Andrew and Roberts, *Final Evaluation Report*, p. 35.

(14) R. Martin and P. Briggs, "Private Firms in the Public Schools," *Education Turnkey News*, 1 (February-March 1971): 2.

(15) Elam, *"Accountability Dawns in Texas,"* p. 509.

(16) The details of this controversy are treated at length in two narratives: Carpenter, Chalfant, and Hall, *Case Studies*, Vol. 3; and Bumstead, R., "Performance Contracting," *Educate*, 3 (October 1970): 15-27.

(17) James Welsh, "D. C. Perspectives on Performance Contracting," *Educational Researcher*, 21 (October 1970): 1. Copyright by American Educational Research Association, Washington, D. C.

(18) For example, see Fred M. Hechinger, "Negative Verdict on a Teaching Program," *New York Times*, February 6, 1972, p. E9; or Kenneth Gehret, "Performance Contracting: How Does It score?" *Christian Science Monitor*, January 3, 1972, p. 9.

(19) R. Bumstead, "Texarkana—The First Accounting," *Educate*, 3 (March 1970): 24-28f; Elam, *Accountability Dawns in Texas*.

(20) L. Lessinger, D. Parnell, and R. Kaufman, *Accountability Policies and Procedures* (New York: Croft, 1971), Four Volumes.

(21) Blaschke is emphasizing his "COST-ED Model," a means to simulate the expenditure patterns in a school system.

VII

Descendants of Texarkana

Overview

During 1970-1971, several school districts attempted performance contract projects. Most projects were planned at the same time as Banneker, and for the same reasons: Texarkana and "accountability." Most of them resembled Texarkana in design.

Several projects dispensed with portions of the procedures that Blaschke and Lessinger advocated. Some did their own testing, some neglected the auditor, some did not hire management support, and several did not institute competitive bidding. However, virtually all projects employed private corporations to teach disadvantaged students for one school year and based payment to the contractor on gains on achievement test scores. Most were federally funded or had other outside assistance.

It should be remembered that performance contracts need not resemble that in Texarkana. During 1970-1971, some variations from Texarkana-like contracts included contracts with teachers instead of private corporations, for subject matter other than reading or mathematics, with student populations other than disadvantaged students, for periods of time other than one year, and with measurements and methods of payment other than paying dollars for student test score gains. But these were exceptions; most of the first generation of contracts resembled the Texarkana contract.

Rumors that circulated at the Denver meeting of the Education Commission of the States in July, 1970, suggested that there would be 150 contracts by fall. Perhaps because of the so-called Texarkana testing scandal, which broke in the midst of that meeting, the actual number of performance contracts eventually was to be more nearly 50.

Portland and Keokuk

With little fanfare, Portland, Oregon, had begun to use Title I funds during the spring and summer of 1970 "to allow teachers or educational equipment vendors to demonstrate new procedures and to accept some degree of financial responsibility for the outcome." (1) Five small, one-semester contracts were worked out, two with teachers, three with technology companies.

Since these went virtually unreported, they had little influence nationally. Nevertheless they represent the first of many departures (Banneker was another) from the Blaschke-Lessinger approach. With no needs assessment, no request for proposals (RFP), no outside evaluator, and no audit, these "performance contracts" merely involved the use of a new kind of contract—one which linked payment to results. They were characterized as "suspenseful." (2) In one, a fourth-grade teacher gambled her paycheck on a double-or-nothing bet. Then she did as other contractors would later do: she created a student incentive system, developed special teaching games and teaching materials, signed learning contracts with each student, and employed three assistants. She was, by the way, more successful than many other contractors! "Her students did slightly better than double their prior rate of reading gain" and "she received $1,325 for five weeks of summer work instead of her regular rate of $650." (3)

In Keokuk, Iowa, Title I funds were used to enable five teachers to visit Texarkana and then to adapt aspects of the program that they considered desirable in their local district. In a summer reading program, the teachers adopted the paying of teachers and aides according to student test performance, and they used student incentives. (4)

Texarkana—Year Two

Texarkana continued its Title VIII program in 1970-1971, after repeating the competitive bidding process and selecting a different contractor. This proved to be Educational Development Laboratory (EDL), a division of the McGraw-Hill Publishing Company. Although Texarkana's 5-year dropout prevention program had several components, once again the performance contract was the one that captured special attention.

In a departure from first year procedures, payment to the contractor was based 75 percent upon standardized achievement tests and relied 25 percent on "criterion-referenced" or "curriculum-based" tests.

The contract with EDL was more expensive than the one with Dorsett, a circumstance which prompted Martin Filagamo, the project director, to remark that "It takes about $125 to $150 to get a grade level increase in reading or math—and there are no short cuts to it." (5) This should come as no surprise when one remembers that Dorsett had charged $80 but spent (by his own testimony) twice what he might receive under the contract.

Even at the higher price, EDL apparently did not stand to make a profit. Performance contracting was a form of advertising. "As long as there is an interest in performance contracting, EDL would like to have between three and six a year, no more," a spokesman for the company said. "As a marketing tool we can't afford performance contracts—their major function is to demonstrate EDL's capabilities." (6)

EDL claimed to be the only company in performance contracting with a good enough record for its system so that it could confidently predict achievement on standardized tests. The criterion tests turned out "Fantastic! We never hoped they would turn out so well." (7) However, its purported record notwithstanding, EDL did poorly on the standardized testing. Less than one-third of the students achieved the promised one year's gain; overall the mean score was .48 years in reading and .31 years in mathematics.

In 1971-1972, Texarkana chose to operate the Rapid Learning Centers without an outside company. (8)

Grand Rapids

The least troubled major performance contract site during 1970-1971 was Grand Rapids, Michigan. It had three contractors. Each performed well enough to be invited back during 1971-1972.

Word of Texarkana reached Norman Weinheimer, superintendent in Grand Rapids, in the spring of 1970. He sent a team to observe there. Impressed by performance contracting, he soon agreed, without competitive bidding, to contracts with Westinghouse Learning Corporation and with Combined Motivation Education Systems (CO/MES). As had Portland, Grand Rapids dispensed with needs assessment, RFPs, competitive bidding, outside evaluation, and audit; it retained only the contract. That summer, Alpha Learning Systems was assigned to Grand Rapids also, as part of the OEO experiment.

For several reasons, Grand Rapids was receptive to performance contracting and yet managed to avoid troubles that arose elsewhere. The Michigan State Superintendent, John Porter, became one of the nation's outspoken advocates of performance contracting and urged its proliferation throughout Michigan. House Minority Leader Gerald Ford, whose Congressional district is Grand Rapids, lent support. The Michigan Education Association and the Grand Rapids Education Association adopted sympathetic wait-and-see attitudes. They said, in effect, if these companies can do what schools have not been able to do, how can we stand in their way. Assistant Superintendent Elmer Vruggink, whose responsibility these programs became, had recently completed a 5-year study of the failure of compensatory education programs. He was sympathetic to new approaches. Pointing to these contracts as examples of desired improvement, he emphasized that

Sometimes in education we have scattered shots. . . . I think we have to zero in on what we're supposed to do. What is successful here may not be *the* system (the contractor uses) but merely being systematic. (9)

Perhaps most important, Joan Webster (who began as Project Director for the OEO contract but expanded her duties to become liaison to all three projects) was a knowledgeable spokeswoman for the approaches of these contractors. She led both the school district and the companies through many of the inevitable rough spots which damaged projects in other cities.

Grand Rapids was less critical than some cities of contractors when they fell short of their guarantees. Even though contractors had overestimated and lost money, they had done better than the school system probably would have done. As a rule, teachers, parents, school administrators, and students were pleased by the "systematic" instruction the three companies had attempted. Considered as promising developing programs, these projects were invited to remain a second year and even to expand.

Westinghouse, for example, had begun with two Learning Centers to teach reading and mathematics to underachieving students within two schools. By February, the two centers had expanded to include all reading and mathematics instruction in the two schools. Faculty of two other schools petitioned the school district to allow them to purchase the Westinghouse system also. Westinghouse, although it did satisfactorily in Grand Rapids, did poorly in three other cities where it was part of the OEO experiment. When Westinghouse lost interest in performance contracts, some of its personnel reincorporated as Learning Unlimited and worked in six Grand Rapids schools during 1971-1972.

Alpha Learning Systems, in Grand Rapids as part of the OEO experiment, found that Grand Rapids was the best project among its three OEO sites. It too expanded in Grand Rapids as well as acquiring contracts in Lansing and Detroit.

CO/MES had the least conventional program of the three; it introduced the practice of "achievement motivation sessions" which every student attended weekly. The presumption was that students who became motivated to learn would learn the CO/MES curriculum. CO/MES was one of several contractors who overpromised in its guarantee and lost money, even though its test scores were twice what would have been expected from these students. The bittersweet irony of performing better than ever before but, less than had been promised, plagued several performance contracts in 1970-1971. CO/MES stayed the second year but planned to cease performance contracting after that.

After 1970-1971, Grand Rapids pictured itself as more sophisticated in the ways of contracting than most districts. The district had learned that performance contracts, since they increase a company's risk, may be more expensive than conventional contracts. Therefore, while Grand Rapids increased the operations of private corporations in the schools in 1971-1972, it used fewer performance contracts. The major success of performance contracts had been to enable the companies involved to sell themselves initially. Had they not evidenced a willingness to "put their money where their mouth was to express confidence in their approach" (10), the district would not have risked hiring them in 1970.

Although Grand Rapids eschewed most of the Blaschke approach to performance contracting, this school district remains the best example of "turnkey" as Blaschke described it. Companies are allowed to demonstrate their abilities by sharing the financial risk in a performance contract; if they perform satisfactorily, part or all of their program is then incorporated into the school system. By 1972 Grand Rapids expects to be using the techniques of these companies without the companies. (11)

Philadelphia

Unlike most performance contracts, BRL supplied materials and teacher training to over 500 Philadelphia teachers but otherwise exercised little control. Essentially, BRL guaranteed the effectiveness of its materials.

Similar to the Grand Rapids project with Combined Motivation Education Systems, the Philadelphia project did better than public schools had done before, but less well than BRL had "guaranteed."

During 1970-1971, Philadelphia committed $600,000 of federal money to a double-or-nothing contract with BRL to teach reading in District 4, a black inner city district. Fifteen thousand students—including all primary grade students plus underachievers in grades 4 to 7—were designated. BRL guaranteed one year's achievement for every child who attended school 150 days or more; no results, no pay. Instead of its usual $20 per student, BRL would receive $40 for each student who succeeded, nothing for others.

Results split in thirds. So did explanations. Approximately one third of the students did not qualify under the minimum attendance clause. Another third achieved the year's gain. The remainder did not. According to the *Philadelphia Inquirer's* front page headline, 65 percent had failed. (12) The school district rebutted this by saying that even though the majority did not make one full year of progress, they had made more progress in that one year than in any previous year. (13) Also, BRL claimed that a mean gain in reading of 0.9 years, for 15,000 students, is "probably the best result ever achieved in an inner city." (14)

Regardless of interpretation of the scores, the drama of the performance contract succeeded in creating public interest in school reading achievement. BRL remained in District 4 with a mixture of fixed- and performance contracts during 1971-1972.

Virginia and Colorado

Learning Research Associates (LRA) had been selected among eight bidders for a seven-month contract in seven Virginia counties. Under the aegis of the State Department of Education, with Title I funding, six rural settings and the inner city of Norfolk (15) involved underachieving students in a tightly structured reading program.

As in Texarkana—Year Two, the contractor received 25 percent of his payment on criterion measures and 75 percent on standardized test scores. LRA suffered the same fate as EDL: it did well on criterion tests and poorly on standardized tests.

Many participants in the project, from classroom teachers to state officials to LRA, struggled to reconcile the impression that students performed well with test scores averaging less than 0.5 years gain. Impressions of success had been bolstered by the annual statewide testing in Virginia which had shown many students advancing one or two years over previous tests; but the LRA posttest scores were much lower.

One possible explanation would be that the standardized test contained items inconsistent with instructional objectives of LRA. Equally telling is the explanation from a spokesman for LRA who said

One thing we will never do again is specify that the testing be done as late as possible. We were naive in testing so late while other kids in the school were having parties and going to picnics. (16)

Virginia decided, like Texarkana, to continue the program without the contractor. Frank Barham, project director in Prince Edward County, evidenced a kind of shrewd patience that is rare among participants in performance contracts:

We believe the instructional phase of this program has merit, is better than anything we have used previously (systematically organized), and with two-three years application, it will tend to increase and upgrade the level of achievement of our pupils. In other words, a good instructional program will not necessarily demonstrate an immediate change in standardized test scores. . . . We believe a few years of concentrated effort with this program will demonstrate the results (achievement gains) so many people may have expected the first year. (17)

Virginia first thought about performance contracting in February, 1970, when first results from Texarkana started the bandwagon rolling. It took ten months. In contrast, the Colorado State Department started in August, 1970, yet began operation before

Virginia. Colorado staff members attended an August conference in Chicago sponsored by Combined Motivation Education Systems and returned home anxious to begin.

For lack of time, Colorado dismissed the preliminaries, designed a small experiment in three cities with 100 junior high students at each site, and selected Dorsett as the contractor.

Denver and two suburban districts agreed to participate and began construction of Rapid Learning Centers. But when word of the Texarkana scandal reached Colorado in September, Denver backed out, forcing the state department to scramble to find a third suburb. Northglenn School District 12 "apparently was so frightened of public reaction to the unpopular concept . . . that it conducted its vote on the Dorsett contract in a secret session." (18)

Loyd Dorsett subsequently claimed he succeeded in getting one year's gain in 80 hours of instruction in each of these sites and is willing to guarantee that to anyone, anywhere. (19)

Others

There were other projects with similar histories, but the pattern becomes repetitive. EDL/McGraw-Hill had contracts in Flint and Muskegon Heights, Michigan, and San Diego; BRL had a small contract in Monroe, Michigan; CO/MES had another in Greenville, South Carolina; LRA had another in Jacksonville; Educational Solutions had them in Boston (20) and Oakland, California; Westinghouse had one in Gilroy, California (21); Webster Division of McGraw-Hill claimed to have two contracts but refused to say where. Occasionally one heard rumors of others, such as those small ones in Portland and Keokuk, which never achieved visibility.

In the summer of 1971, the American Federation of Teachers focused attention on the teaching-the-test problem by pinpointing purported wrongdoing in Providence, Rhode Island. The contractor, New Century, had introduced a new textbook which contained a very high coincidence with test items, just two weeks prior to the post-test. Nevertheless, the scores were low and New Century lost money.

Notes

(1) J. N. Holmes, "Performance Contracting," Portland Public Schools, November 6, 1970. (mimeographed)
(2) Ibid.
(3) J. Guernsey, "Daring Teacher Gambles Pay on Reading," *The Oregonian,* November 12, 1970.
(4) J. D. Reynolds, "Performance Contracting . . . Proceed With Caution," *The English Journal,* 60 (January 1971): 102-106f.
(5) "Texarkana: The Second Year Around," *Nation's Schools,* 87 (March 1971): 33.
(6) Stated by John Dungan in a telephone interview with the author, August 2, 1971.
(7) Ibid.
(8) The most extensive treatment of the second year in Texarkana is in P. Carpenter, A. W. Chalfant, and G. R. Hall, *Case Studies in Educational Performance*

Contracting, Volume 3, *Texarkana, Arkansas, and Liberty Eylau, Texas* (Santa Monica: Rand, 1971), pp. 36ff. McGraw-Hill's intentions were expressed by Edmund Zazzera, president of EDL, in "A Contractor's Viewpoint," *Compact,* 5 (February 1971): 13-16.

(9) Stated by Elmer Vruggink in an interview with the author, in St. Louis, Missouri, April 8, 1971.

(10) Ibid.

(11) More extensive treatments of the Grand Rapids projects can be found in J. A. Mecklenburger, and J. A. Wilson, "The Performance Contracts in Grand Rapids," *Phi Delta Kappan,* 51 (June 1971): 590-594; B. Asbell, "Should Private Enterprise Direct Your Child's Education?", *Redbook,* 37 (February 1972): 56-60; G. C. Sumner, *Case Studies in Educational Performance Contracting,* Volume 6, *Grand Rapids, Michigan* (Santa Monics: Rand, 1971).

(12) H. S. Shapiro and T. Hine, "65% Fail City's Contract Reading Plan," *Philadelphia Inquirer,* August 20, 1971.

(13) F. Hamilton, "School District to Continue 'Project Read'," *Philadelphia Daily News,* August 25, 1971, citing an interview with Ruth Hayre, District Superintendent of District #4.

(14) C. Blaschke, "Performance Contracting," *Nation's Schools,* 88 (October 1971): 19, citing Roger R. Sullivan, President of Behavioral Research Laboratories.

(15) The only published extensive analysis of Virginia's project is P. Carpenter, *Case Studies in Educational Performance Contracting,* Volume 2, *Norfolk, Virginia* (Santa Monica: Rand, 1971).

(16) C. Rice, "Evaluating Virginia's Performance Contract Program," *Virginia Journal of Education,* 65 (September 1971): 14.

(17) Personal letter written by Frank E. Barham to the author, July 26, 1971.

(18) "Performance Contract Broker Calls Some Contracts Illegal," *American Teacher,* 55 (April 1971): 7.

(19) Stated by Loyd Dorsett, in a panel on performance contracting at the American Association of School Administrators, Atlantic City, February 15, 1972.

(20) Described in E. Sigel and M. Sobel, *Accountability and the Controversial Role of the Performance Contractors,* Knowledge Industry Publications, 1971, pp. 25-28, 77-78.

(21) See M. L. Rapp, *Case Studies in Educational Performance Contracting,* Volume 5, *Gilroy, California* (Santa Monica: Rand, 1971).

VIII

Texarkana
Times Eighteen—
The OEO Experiment

Overview

Overshadowing every performance contract except Texarkana and Banneker is the experiment conducted by the Office of Economic Opportunity during 1970-1971. OEO, too, adopted the model of hiring private educational technology companies to teach basic skills to disadvantaged students. Payment was geared to "guaranteed" test score gains as determined by an outside evaluator administering standardized achievement tests. OEO heightened the drama of performance contracting by pitting six companies against each other as well as against conventional teaching, and by pitting itself against the "educational establishment" of NEA, AFT, and the U. S. Office of Education.

The OEO experiment, like Banneker and Texarkana, began as a development effort for the companies involved. As at Banneker and Texarkana there was confusion over roles, high public visibility, and some serious problems that simmered beneath the public image created by OEO.

In February, 1972, OEO seriously damaged the reputation and potential of performance contracting by announcing it to be "clearly another failure."

The Politics
of the OEO Experiment

OEO consciously imitated (some would say capitalized upon) what appeared to be the new "panacea" in Texarkana. Says OEO, its decision to experiment came as "great enthusiasm and optimism greeted reports that a new program, called performance contracting, was succeeding beyond anyone's wildest hopes with poor children in Texarkana, Arkansas. . . ." (1) OEO found performance contracting an attractive concept because of its emphasis on outputs, its promise for aiding poor children, and "indications that performance contracting would become a fad." (2)

OEO staff members visited Texarkana and "saw great promise in performance contracting."

But they also realized that the Texarkana project was not designed to provide adequate guidance for the dozens of other school districts that were considering the new concept. . . . It was not an experiment with a rigorous evaluation structure. . . . It was clear, then, that a much broader, clearly defined, and carefully evaluated experience was necessary before it could be confidently stated that performance contracting could help poor children learn. (3)

A year and a half later, OEO tried to wash its hands of performance contracting.

OEO did not act merely out of the goodness of its heart. Charles Stalford and Jeffry Schiller, of the OEO staff, had visited Texarkana, had been intrigued by what they saw and were told. They came back to Washington recommending that an experiment with this concept would coincide with the OEO commission to do important social research. The decision to act upon their recommendation, according to Stalford, carried through the chain of command to the White House and back again. (4) This is important to bear in mind since, from its beginning, the project existed on two levels, political and experimental. In a sense, two lessons had been extracted from Texarkana: that performance contracting squared with President Nixon's administration policy and could be exploited to further that policy, and that performance contracting might hold a key to improving the education of poor children. One cannot help but be reminded of Blaschke's contention that programs are usually sold on the basis of political, social, and economic merits and later justified on educational grounds.

Announcement of the project revealed its political value: it promised to appease the poor, to provide better education for no more money, to challenge the teacher organizations that demanded more money, and do all this in the name of free enterprise and scientific experiment! Neither NEA nor AFT had been consulted about this project, nor for that matter had Leon Lessinger, "the father of accountability." Rather, the project had been intruded as a political coup, jabbing the prestige of the NEA, AFT, and Office of Education simultaneously. It struck directly at the oft heard argument from these sources that the fundamental answer to educational improvement is more money, especially more federal money. John O. Wilson, OEO Assistant Director for Planning, Research, and Evaluation, announced the project in July:

Various educational innovations that show great promise are being developed by private industry. . . . In effect, the techniques promise that for the first time, education will be able to promise "equality of results"; that ways can be found to bring poor children up to a level of achievement comparable to that of their nonpoor classmates, and that those providing the education will not be paid if "equality of results" is not provided. (5)

"From the standpoint of potential educational reform," said Donald Rumsfeld, Director of OEO, in September, 1970, "the most significant feature of this concept is accountability: no success, no pay." (6) He added:

Contractors are paid only to the extent that they are successful in improving the educational skills of the children they instruct. In the experiment, the contractors will be paid only if they increase skills by more than one grade level. They will make a profit only if skills increase by 1.6 grade levels, nearly four times the average now attained in schools serving poor neighborhoods. (7)

Rumsfeld and his successors Frank Carlucci and Philip Sanchez each found themselves hammering the political significance of the OEO "experiment." Rumsfeld's September speech remains the most eloquent:

One would expect that news of the experiments would be greeted with enthusiasm among educators who for years have been voicing their concern about education and the poor. Interestingly, this has not been the case. Lobbyists for the education special interest groups have used most of the means at their disposal to attack the experiments. . . . I find it strange that individuals who claim to be dedicated to advancing the frontiers of learning oppose legitimate efforts to improve methods of transmitting knowledge to children.

Let there be no doubt about it—a major effort has been mounted by a handful of self-appointed education spokesmen to halt any inquiry into the possibility of educational reform. . . .

They fear experimentation because it may call into question their dogmas and orthodoxies. . . . I doubt that these people speak for most teachers. . . . I'm sure that many teachers, like many professionals in other fields, are frustrated by the rigidities of their professional organizations. The best of these teachers are not afraid to experiment; they avidly seek new knowledge and new methods. They reject the rule of the mediocre, which now seems to characterize some professional interest groups. . . . (8)

The mood in the early weeks of the OEO project was captured in the "Washington News" pages of *Education Digest:*

The Office of Economic Opportunity has awarded 18 contracts of this kind that are hailed, of course, as harbingers of the future, even before they have been completed and evaluated. . . . The evaluations are likely to be glowing ones; the OEO has never funded an evaluation of its programs that found any to be wanting. (9)

Albert Shanker, president of the New York United Federation of

Teachers, asserted that the OEO experiment was "phony." "This isn't viewed as an experiment, it's a juggernaut. Everyone's going around saying it will succeed." (10)

In order to justify the positive tone of its rhetoric—that is, to conduct an experiment as if it were a demonstration—OEO stressed the cost-effectiveness of contractors' programs (Blaschke's firm was hired to gather the necessary data to prove this), the scientific quality of the OEO evaluation, and the capabilities of the educational technology companies. The evidence for this last attribute was the willingness of the companies to guarantee success.

To avoid unpleasant contradiction, OEO required that no information be released by schools and contractors unless first cleared through OEO. Thus, with scattered exceptions in AFT publications and local newspapers, no information was available to counteract the public image of this experiment. (11)

Nevertheless, as the winds of political fortune would have it, OEO took tremendous criticism over this project, and even more over its sister project, the educational voucher. From the summer of 1970 until the winter of 1971-1972, the OEO star plummeted in the Washington firmament, reaching a low ebb in December, 1971, when President Nixon vetoed the OEO appropriation (as part of the Mondale child care bill he vetoed) and announced his intention to give OEO a "new role."

Preliminary results of the OEO experiment had been promised in the summer of 1971, but they were delayed month after month and finally released January 31, 1972, only after Seattle had sued OEO for the information. Coincident with that release, *Saturday Review* remarked that the OEO programs are not likely to make political waves in an election year. . . . For its part, OEO is no longer pulling rabbits out of hats. It is consolidating, regrouping, trying to survive." The article quotes John O. Wilson as follows:

With performance contracting and vouchers we get rapidly into the area of institutional change. We tested the water, got new ideas into the arena, forced people to think of alternatives. We went after high visibility. Of course, we didn't want our visibility to be *that* high. (12)

In these circumstances, the OEO decision as to how to couch the release of data was highly colored by political considerations. OEO needed a victory.

In its release of results to the press, January 31, 1972, OEO featured an earlier remark by Donald Rumsfeld, director of OEO, to preface its report:

If the results prove that all the approaches that we utilize within the umbrella of the total experiment are not successful and not desirable, the evaluation will indicate that. By the same token, the experiment still will affect policy because it will lead us to the conclusion that performance contracting is not a desirable route to go. (13)

OEO would save political face by claiming success of its experimentation while regretting that performance contracting had failed. Therefore OEO unequivocally condemned performance contracting:

The single most important question for all concerned with the experiment is: Was performance contracting more successful than traditional classroom methods in improving the reading and math skills of poor children. The answer is: No.

While we judge this experiment to be a success in terms of the information it can offer about the capabilities of performance contractors, it is clearly another failure in our search for means of helping poor and disadvantaged youngsters to develop the skills they need to lift themselves out of poverty. (14)

This stance allowed OEO to claim a $7 million investment in the public welfare. On the heels of the eagerness of OEO to wash its hands of performance contracting, NEA and AFT quickly concurred with the OEO condemnation.

In its report, OEO observed that, overall, contractors and school systems tested equally—no significant difference. On this basis, OEO said, performance contracting failed to be the panacea OEO had sought. OEO did not admit to the possibility that OEO itself might have been at fault.

OEO had in its possession a report by the project directors (the eighteen individuals who worked as liaison to the contractors in each school system) which raised questions about flaws in the experiment itself. OEO received this early in January. The project directors had been led to believe their report would be released in January, but OEO must have thought it impolitic to release its own conclusions and this skeptical report simultaneously. The report was postponed. Similarly, the interim evaluation report of Battelle Memorial Institute contains criticisms of OEO; although dated January 29, it was not released until several days after the OEO report. The effect of delayed publication was that nationwide news coverage (and Congressional briefings) carried only the OEO version.

The Design and Weaknesses of the OEO Experiment

Even without the remarks of the Project Directors (see p. 85), several flaws in the OEO experiment are apparent.

OEO selected six small educational technology companies and it selected eighteen cities from Maine to Alaska, urban and rural, with student populations of varying ethnic and racial composition. OEO assigned each company to use its unique instructional approach in three cities.

In its request for proposals, issued in mid-April for a May 11th deadline, OEO outlined its intention: in each city, the contractor would be assigned 600 "underachieving" students, 100 in each of six grades—grades 1, 2, 3 and 7, 8, 9. OEO selected a comparable population that would receive conventional instruction. The same standardized achievement test would be administered nationwide to all "experimental" and "control" students in September and in May. Analysis of pretest and posttest scores would determine the contractor(s) whose methods were most successful.

As in Texarkana, many companies bid, and for the same reasons: hoped-for success in this project might lead to many more lucrative contracts. Since it was clear that OEO would select the companies on the basis of uniqueness of approach, reasonableness of budget, and the grade-level achievement promised, it should be no surprise that the winning proposals were those that had told OEO what it had wanted to hear. OEO presumed with unjustified optimism that the six companies it selected were capable of implementing, in three cities, on short notice, the six programs they proposed. Not only was this naive in terms of the time-squeeze companies would be in, but OEO attended only to the proposals and did not investigate the capacity of these companies to do what OEO had requested.

Though the OEO rhetoric spoke of educational innovations that show great promise being developed by private industry, OEO hired companies whose proposed techniques 1) were not particularly unusual (in reality, it turned out, at some sites the company program closely resembled what the public schools already were doing); 2) generally had not been developed by the companies OEO hired (or even by private industry at all); and 3) were approaches with which these six companies themselves had little or no experience. (See p. 83 for precis of approaches of the six companies.)

Similarly, although OEO accepted as evidence of company capability a willingness to "guarantee" grade-level increases, it apparently did not realize that this was something these companies had never before attempted. The OEO and many others were reacting to the alleged test gains in Texarkana. To get an OEO contract, a company would have to "guarantee" similar gains—which these six companies did. Political spokesmen apparently accepted the company predictions as tantamount to success. Hence Donald Rumsfeld asserted that companies would not even be paid until they did two to four times as well as one expects of public schools. (16)

In fact, the proposals—both instructional techniques and grade-level promises—contained large measures of hope as well as naivete. Unfortunately the six companies were inexperienced in operating such services in a public school setting. Three had experience operating tutorial centers in such sites as shopping centers where parents bring students for remedial instruction; one was a small publisher and developer of instructional materials; one was a

Description of Contractors' Approaches (15)

Alpha Learning Systems   This company minimizes the use of teaching machines; it uses programmed texts and reorganized existing materials. It utilizes an intensive incentive system for both students and teachers. The incentives to students are geared to whatever interests them, be it material gifts, trading stamps, time off, or whatever. Additionally, the learning environment itself is changed with the addition of carpeting and draperies and a separate room used for relaxation.

Singer/Graflex, Inc.   This company uses some teaching machines and audio-visual material and paraprofessionals, in addition to professional teachers. This approach calls for intensive use of incentives to students, teachers, parents, and schools.

Westinghouse Learning Corporation   This company's approach involves a moderate use of teaching machines, tape cassettes, other audio-visual materials, and programmed texts. A unique feature of this approach is the involvement of computer managed instruction and a totally individualized, behaviorally based program. That is, according to performance on diagnostic tests, the computer or managed instruction system prescribes the student's lessons and materials to be used. Extensive use is made of individual behavioral objectives. Material incentives to students are an integral part of this approach. Additionally, the learning environment is modified to reflect a much more relaxed and less institutional atmosphere.

Quality Educational Development   This contractor will employ fairly heavy use of audio-visual teaching machines and tape cassettes as programmed texts. Material incentives will be provided for students and teachers according to student performance.

Learning Foundations   This company's approach involves an extremely heavy use of auto-tutor teaching machines. Paraprofessionals, rather than certified teachers, are employed to monitor students' performance. Also, incentives that gradually change from extrinsic and tangible to intrinsic and attitudinal in nature will be given to students and teachers. Computerized prescribed instruction is also used.

Plan Education Centers   This company's approach employs very little hardware and very few extrinsic incentives to students. The contract uses programmed texts and existing instructional materials and believes that incentives are intrinsic to the learning system. Heavy reliance is placed on diagnostic testing and placement.

government contractor for Job Corps centers, and one a newly formed company whose major effort had been teacher training seminars. Only after they got the contract did they determine the details of how they might work things out.

The OEO final report emphasized that the purpose of the experiment was to evaluate the relative effectiveness of existing techniques, rather than to underwrite the development of new techniques. This was Gary's naive expectation at Banneker also, relying upon the BRL proposal. Yet the following item from *Edubusiness,* an education and training market newsletter, makes clear the discrepancy between what OEO said it was doing, and what the companies it hired intended:

The firms chosen for the $6.5 million OEO school performance contract are almost unanimous on one point—if they make money, it will be very little. The project is a means of advertising and proving the worth of their systems and an opportunity for some intensive research and development.

"We're doing it for the reputation," says Dr. Adrian Parmeter, head of Quality Education Development, one of the winning companies. . . . The value, he thinks, is that schools will begin looking for learning systems, thus opening a market that has been hard to crack. (17)

With companies doing "intensive research and development," the fundamental drama of pitting six unique industry techniques against public school methods proved to be more rhetoric than reality. Furthermore, as the companies developed systems at their sites, they bore a strong resemblance to one another. (Of course, given the OEO description of contractors' proposals, they were similar at the start.)

Also, timing put the contractors at a great disadvantage. (18) Whereas conventional schools hire staff in the spring for jobs to which they are accustomed, contractors were forced during mid-summer to hire unknown staff for innovative programs. School districts had no particular incentive to assist the contractors, and some did not, forcing some contractors to hire whoever was available. (19) Companies had less than eight weeks between the time they signed contracts and the opening of school. This was precious little time in which to hire and train staff, acquire materials, and organize programs as well as to establish a national communications network. (Alpha Learning Systems, for example, with offices in Albuquerque had projects in Texas, Michigan, and Connecticut.) To complicate matters, school districts were supposed to appoint project directors, arrange for classrooms to be refurbished to contractor specifications, and reschedule other school programs and staff in order to accommodate the OEO. Summer vacation hindered all this effort. In fact, several sites were not operational until late September and October, and a few did not operate according to plan until December. Because contractors were developing, not demonstrating their instructional systems, students in regular public school classrooms generally received more well prepared instruction during the first semester than did the "experimental" students.

Ironically, in several ways the OEO had managed its experiment so that its own expectations were thwarted. The Office demanded too much, too fast, while telling the world that this would be a show of business expertise.

Although the OEO Project Directors, in a report submitted January 11, 1972, were circumspect in their wording, their remarks pinpoint problems aggravated by OEO:

All of these problem areas center around a lack of *sufficient time:*
  Late preplanning;
  Lack of local district personnel involvement;
  Late selection of Testing and Analysis Contractor;
  Inadequate preservice training of local staffs.
There is and has been conjecture on the part of many, particularly those agencies who fund programs of this nature, about the trade off between a long lead time to do sufficient planning and a short lead time which forces the "systems" to not become involved in the processes involved. It is the concensus of the Project Directors involved that the former would have been the preferred procedure.

Project Directors questioned the inclusion of first grade students in a remedial program of this type. Readiness programs were lacking and had to be designed by the staffs.

As the programs progressed it appeared that each company did not have an individual or unique curriculum approach. This is supported by the fact that many companies used the same or similar core instructional materials.

It is recommended that maximum effort be made by outside agencies to understand and to function within the strictures placed upon local districts by states and by other authorities beyond the local district's control.

It is recommended that ongoing evaluation be specified and criteria for acceptable performance be defined with contract cancellation if minimal performance lines are not maintained at established check points.

Lines of communication in an experiment of such magnitude must be an area of major concern and effort. . . . When a conference was called at the conclusion of the project, Project Directors were amazed to find the universality of the problems they had encountered. (20)

In sum, OEO had not done several managerial things one might reasonably expect in such an effort. The OEO itself was primarily responsible for unsatisfactory efforts at pretesting, training staff, organizing nationally, and avoiding conflicts of regulations.

Table 2 summarizes data across all sites for the OEO experiment. On the basis of several analyses of these data, OEO said, "It is fairly clear that regardless of the perspective taken, performance contracting was not responsible for any significant improvement on an overall basis." (22)

OEO might well have asked a more interesting question: Among

TABLE 2

Mean Gains of Experimental and Control Students
Across All Sites[21]

	Reading		
	Experimental Gain	Control Gain	Difference
Grade 1	NA	NA	NA
2	.4	.5	-.1
3	.3	.2	+.1
7	.4	.3	+.1
8	.9	1.0	-.1
9	.8	.8	--

	Math		
	Experimental Gain	Control Gain	Difference
Grade 1	NA	NA	NA
2	.5	.5	--
3	.4	.4	--
7	.6	.6	--
8	.8	1.0	-.2
9	.8	.8	--

NA: A readiness test, rather than an achievement test, was used as the first grade pretest. There is no grade equivalent for the readiness test.

the 18 sites, was there *any* evidence of successful teaching, or grossly unsuccessful teaching, on the part of contractors, which would reveal new knowledge about teaching underachieving students? Nothing in its report was addressed to this question. One reporter at the press conference asked if any specific sites had been relatively successful, and learned to his surprise that five had been and that one contractor had achieved nearly his full payment at one site. There had also been a few very unsuccessful sites. OEO brushed both success and failure beneath a statistical rug.

OEO neglected to mention that in terms of some of its own earlier criteria, its experiment had been fruitful. First, Donald Rumsfeld had said "the most significant feature of this concept is accountability: no success, no pay." (23) That is, performance contracting would make it possible to reward according to the results of instruction. By this criterion, performance contracting succeeded, for contractors were indeed paid according to the results as determined by the use of agreed upon measures. Second, OEO had emphasized performance contracting as a means to discover most cost-effective instructional techniques. Blaschke succeeded in demonstrating that, even with modest achievement scores, some OEO contractors had instructional systems which were more cost-effective than conventional instruction. (24) Third, in some cities, notably Grand Rapids but also in five others, (25) some aspects of the contractors' programs later were incorporated into the schools.

A number of statistical questions may be raised with respect to the results of the OEO experiment. Battelle Memorial Institute, as outside evaluator, rejected the use of grade equivalent scores for evaluative purposes because they "possess psychometric distortions which might affect the results of statistical analyses." (26) Yet OEO reported only grade equivalent scores. Secondly, Battelle rejected comparison of pretest and posttest mean scores of experimental and control groups because "it does not provide a quantitative adjustment in mean posttest differences due to mean pretest differences." (27) Again OEO stressed this kind of comparison.

Comparison of means, as shown in Table 2, can be highly misleading when no information is reported concerning range, distribution, or standard deviation of scores. It would obviously be possible, for example, for "experimental" scores to range widely while "control" scores cluster around the mean, or vice versa. These events would suggest very different interpretations, even though mean scores were identical.

OEO admits that test data from individual sites lacked reliability, due to many factors, such as Battelle's enforced haste. Battelle confirms this in its own report. (28) Yet, says OEO, if one sums up all the data, "these problems do, for the most part, offset each other in the overall comparisons." (29) This is a dubious generalization, for if individual scores are questionable, generalizations about them patently cannot be less questionable.

In view of the above analysis it appears that for several reasons—some political, some statistical, some based on observation of the experiment itself—the claim of OEO to a successful experiment which yields clear answers simply is not justified.

Notes

(1) Office of Economic Opportunity, "An Experiment in Performance Contracting—Summary of Preliminary Results," OEO Pamphlet #3400-5, p. 2. Released at press conference, January 31, 1972; dated February, 1972.
(2) Ibid., Appendix, "Why Undertake the Experiment."
(3) John O. Wilson, "Performance Contracting — An Experiment in Accountability," mimeographed press release, undated, pp. 2-3.
(4) Stated by Charles Stalford, in an interview with the author at Elkridge, Maryland, December 10, 1971.
(5) John O. Wilson, press release, July, 1970; reprinted in *Congressional Record,* 92nd Congress:S11407-8, July 15, 1970.
(6) Donald Rumsfeld, in an address to the Urban Roundtable of the San Francisco Chamber of Commerce, September 23, 1970.
(7) Ibid.
(8) Ibid.
(9) Theodore Schuchat, *Education Digest,* November, 1970, p. 57.

(10) E. Sigel and M. Sobel, *Accountability and the Controversial Role of the Performance Contractors,* Knowledge Industry Publications, 1971, p. 42, citing an interview with Albert Shanker.

(11) The OEO public depiction of performance contracts as the harbinger of the future would have been more credible had OEO not announced its program based on the Texarkana project days before the teaching-the-test scandal greeted Texarkana. One wonders whether the OEO project might not have quietly disappeared if the Texarkana scandal had broken first. Except to point out that their experiment took extraordinary pains to avoid teaching-the-test, OEO understandably ignored the Texarkana fracas, although critics and skeptics continually remembered.

(12) P. Janssen, "OEO as Innovator," *Saturday Review,* 55 (February 5, 1972): 43, citing an interview with John O. Wilson. Copyright 1972 *Saturday Review, Inc.*

(13) Office of Economic Opportunity, "Experiment in Performance Contracting," frontispiece.

(14) Ibid., pp. 17, 32.

(15) Wilson, press release, July, 1970.

(16) Rumsfeld, op. cit.

(17) "Special Report: OEO Performance Contract," *Edubusiness,* August 6, 1970.

(18) It has been suggested that six months is a minimum amount of lead time. According to Charles Blaschke, "While it takes about six months to plan one performance contract project, OEO total start-up time was about two and a half to three months for 18." (Blaschke, C. "Performance Contracting: Who Profits Most?" Quotations are from an unedited manuscript, much of which was subsequently published. See Charles Blaschke, *Performance Contracting: Who Profits Most?* Bloomington, Indiana: Phi Delta Kappa Educational Foundation, 1972.) In Daniel M. Layer, "Here's How to Get Ready for the Contract," *American School Board Journal,* 159 (October 1971): 33, six months is also the recommended lead time for a single contract. In *Guaranteed Performance Contracting,* Lansing, 1971, the Michigan Department of Education recommends nine months lead time for a single contract. Texarkana required 9 months, Banneker 6 months, and Virginia (with 7 contracts, but 1 contractor) took 10 months.

(19) During his summer vacation in mid-August, 1970, the author chanced to meet a contractor's representative who would have hired him on the spot to begin work the next day. In order to recruit staff so late in the summer, he was running newspaper help wanted notices; the school system would release no staff to that project.

(20) "Project Directors' Evaluation," unpublished report submitted to the Office of Economic Opportunity by the twenty Project Directors, January 11, 1972.

Battelle Memorial Institute received its contract with OEO on August 10, 1970, only two weeks before it would find itself testing in 18 cities. As Battelle describes in its "Interim Report," submitted to OEO January 29, 1972 (*The Office of Economic Opportunity Experiment in Educational Performance Contracting,* Battelle Memorial Institute, Columbus, Ohio, January 29, 1972), Battelle's short lead time caused severe problems with the overall quality of the pretests.

(21) Office of Economic Opportunity, "Experiment in Performance Contracting," p. 18.

(22) Ibid., p. 19.

(23) Rumsfeld, op. cit.

(24) C. Blaschke, "Performance Contracting Costs, Management Reform and John Q. Citizen," *Phi Delta Kappan,* 53 (December 1971): 245-7.

(25) C. Blaschke, "The OEO Project Results," press release, February 1, 1972.

(26) Battelle Memorial Institute, op. cit., p. 10.

(27) Ibid., p. 62.

(28) Ibid., pp. 46-53.

(29) Office of Economic Opportunity, "Experiment in Performance Contracting," p. 22.

IX

Alternatives
to the Texarkana Model

Most educators do not devote much attention to contracts. Characteristically, schools use only one category of contract, a fixed-price contract for services. In it, for a set fee, teachers contract to teach, administrators to administer, counselors to counsel, and so forth. Contracts—like the five-day week or the A-B-C-D-F grading scale—have become a part of the school culture where they are largely taken for granted.

Conventional vs. Performance Contracts

It does seem suitable for schools to contract for best efforts, since most schools perceive themselves as providing their professional efforts toward appropriate ends. But no one thought much about the suitability of contracts until the arrival of performance contracts. Their emphasis on contracting for results (instead of for effort) brought contracting out of seclusion and exposed it to public scrutiny.

Because many people expect results from schooling, performance contracts represent an emphasis which has widespread appeal. Recent polls among teachers, school board members, school administrators, and the general public have revealed one- to two-thirds of respondents sympathetic to some form of performance contracting in schools. (1)

In emphasizing results, performance contracts are not isolated phenomena. Rather, they participate in a groundswell of educational ideas and practices which emphasize results. Management by objectives, performance planning and budgeting, educational accomplishment audits, programmed instruction, contingency management, curricula geared to behavioral objectives, cost/benefit analysis, competency-based teacher education, voucher plans (sometimes called "performance contracting with parents"), differentiated staffing, criterion-referenced testing and other notions share with performance contracting a results-oriented perspective. "Instructional technology," "systems approaches," and especially "accountability" are terms sometimes loosely applied to this agglomeration. Polls indicate a still higher percentage of favor, among the public and educators, for some form of "accountability." (2) Whatever terminology survives, as long as result-oriented ideas and practices have currency, performance contracting is likely to be among them.

The Texarkana Model

Because of its historical importance during 1969-1971, this book has emphasized the Texarkana model and its offspring. However, in the judgement of the author, the Texarkana model of performance contracting will probably decline in popularity.

The seeds of its own destruction are already evident in its history: 1) high risk for low profits; 2) extra teacher and administrative effort in uncomfortable new roles; 3) conflict with powerful political forces; 4) inadequate use of evaluation tools; 5) an exaggerated public image, and 6) the failure of such contracts to fulfill the expectations that image invites.

The OEO was correct in this: Texarkana-like contracts are no panacea. Since they are not, those who seek panaceas will need to look elsewhere. That this is already happening is suggested by the fact that there were only a dozen performance contracts during 1971-1972 as compared to fifty the year before.

RAND was also correct, however: contracts can be effective change agents which help both schools and companies to *develop* better instructional programs. For this reason, Texarkana-like contracts may not be popular but probably will not disappear.

Other Permutations

In Texarkana-like contracts, "results" have been narrowly equated with standardized test scores. But in thinking about the possibilities for performance contracts, test scores are something of a red herring. *Any* results that can be specified can be contracted, whether academic attainments, dropout prevention, vocational skills, teacher competencies, achievement motivation, athletic abilities, student satisfaction, or college admission, to name a few.

To date, contracts primarily have served disadvantaged students. However, performance contracting (like differentiated staffing or behavioral objectives) is a device which might serve any population in public or private schools—elementary, secondary, higher education, prekindergarten, achieving, or underachieving.

Although one school year has been a convenient length of time for contracts, any time span might be suitable. Banneker is for four years. Virginia was for seven months. Portland was for one semester and then for one summer session.

Most performance contracts have been between school districts and private corporations, but any two (or more) parties could sign a performance contract.

Finally, although Texarkana-like performance contracts have linked "payment" to results by linking dollars to test scores, "payment" might be stock options (as Dorsett offered his teachers in Texarkana), prizes, bonuses, vacations, privileges, guaranteed contract renewal, or anything else of value.

Undoubtedly there will be new terminology. Roald Campbell has suggested "pupil achievement contract" as a more accurate term. (3) Others refer to "teacher support contracts" or "incentive contracts" as different from "conventional performance contracts."

Stockton and Mesa

Portland and Keokuk had signed performance contracts with individual teachers and with small clusters of teachers. As part of its national experiment, in addition to contracting with educational technology companies, OEO planned to sign performance contracts with three education associations which were NEA affiliates.

These experiments were intended to test whether teachers who could give incentives to students, and who received incentives themselves for student achievement, would perform better than conventional teachers.

One of the three possible sites considered was Grand Rapids. However the teachers there voted to reject the OEO invitation since it would have placed them "in a sort of quasi-competition with the three learning corporations" in Grand Rapids. (4) In November, 1970, OEO settled for two teacher contracts, one in Stockton, California, the other in Mesa, Arizona.

These were hastily implemented experiments, even more so than the eighteen contracts with companies. According to the report by the two project directors, (5) the contracts were not signed until November and the experiment began in December. Selecting 600 experimental and 600 control students in each city, testing them, and rearranging school schedules to accomodate the experiment, caused ill-feeling which carried into the experiment.

Prior to the OEO report of its experiment with performance contracting, a few statements by the two project directors and by OEO officials had indicated some benefit and pleasure with the Mesa and Stockton projects. But at the January 31st press conference, OEO dismissed Stockton and Mesa as still more cases of no significant difference between experimental and control groups.

It is hard to separate the experimental purposes of OEO, or even its demonstration purposes, from the political intentions associated with the Mesa and Stockton projects. One immediate political effect was to soften NEA criticism of performance contracting and of OEO. Had the initial expectations of OEO been fulfilled—that project schools would outdistance conventional schools—these contracts would have (presumably) demonstrated that teachers would still not be as effective as private corporations.

Speaking nonpolitically, Charles Stalford, OEO project director, once remarked that the use of incentives in Stockton and Mesa "may turn out to be like the Wright Brothers." (6) He could prove correct; certainly contracting with teachers for results has more potential for growth than contracting with private corporations, if only because there are so many more teachers, and because teachers already negotiate contracts with schools. One of the early contracts in Portland, Oregon, was a contract between the school system and teachers who then subcontracted with a private corporation. Possibilities are numerous.

Duval County and Dallas

Virtually every contract, 1969-1971, was for reading or for reading and mathematics instruction. But there were exceptions: Banneker involved the entire curriculum, although it stressed reading and mathematics achievement. The contract in Duval County, Florida, with Learning Research Associates (LRA) involved first grade teachers who taught the entire curriculum. Dallas held a contract for vocational education and achievement motivation with the Clearfield Division of Thiokol Chemical Company. (7)

In the Duval County Project IMPACT, emphasis was placed on teacher training. The school district determined that teachers should be trained in the use of "inquiry" or "scientific heuristic" methods of instruction. Moreover, the school system selected the teaching materials to be used.

LRA was termed the "teacher support contractor." The program began in winter of 1970-1971 and ended in June; it was refunded for 1971-1972 and anticipated operating for two more years. In the first phase, only first grade teachers participated. They received three weeks of preservice training and LRA continued to assist and train teachers throughout the program. In the second year, the trained first-grade teachers became second-grade teachers (with further assistance from LRA). They, in turn, aided a new group of first-grade teachers.

The presumption behind the Duval County contract was that better trained teachers would improve student performance. Therefore, payment to the contractor was based on several measures of student achievement:

1) Fifty percent of the contractor's payment required that the mean achievement of the experimental students exceed the mean achievement of a random sample of other Title I students.
2) Twenty-five percent of the payment was based on criterion-referenced tests in curriculum areas of reading, mathematics, social studies and science.
3) Twenty percent was based on student achievement above expectation in reading, mathematics, science, and social studies.
4) Five percent was based on gains in IQ scores.

In the first phase, the contractor received approximately 70 percent of his possible income.

In Dallas, a year before the vocational and motivation experiment began, planning commenced with a city-wide planning team of parents, businessmen, civic leaders, and teachers. One highlight of this group effort was inclusion of a course in drafting for girls. Every graduate of this course was later employed by local industry. The planning group prepared a Request for Proposals, and Thiokol was selected in competitive bidding.

Increased school attendance in reading and mathematics classes was the measure of Thiokol's success in achievement motivation. Also, Thiokol was required to keep dropout rates below those of other Title VIII projects. Although all students were initially identified as potential dropouts, 91 percent remained in school and their attendance increased to 86 percent average from 73 percent the previous year. Though not reflected in payment to Thiokol, students who attended achievement motivation sessions performed better on reading and mathematics tests than students who did not.

Vocational training success was judged in terms of "employability" which was measured both by actual employment (26.7 percent of students) or judgement by a panel of employers that a student would qualify for employment. Employability was achieved by 57.7 percent at the level of apprentice, assistant, or helper.

Dallas insisted that contractors' programs be compatible with the operation of the school system, and use persons already on the school system staff. This was done so that successful programs could be "turnkeyed," that is, made an integral part of the permanent program. The Thiokol program was turnkeyed in 1971-1972.

Cherry Creek's I-Team

I-Team, where "I" stands for interdisciplinary, was a dropout prevention program developed under Title VIII. In 1970-1971, students were high school juniors and seniors identified by counselors as potential dropouts. These students were encouraged to volunteer for I-Team.

Although partially an academic program, I-Team was reminiscent of free schools and street academies elsewhere. Unlike the conventional high school in Cherry Creek, Colorado, the I-Team was small, relaxed, personal, and student-centered. Academic work was divided into "mini-courses" tailored to student interests; while some students chose to pursue a traditional course of study, others did not. But there was also time available for lounging and relaxing, for counseling and small-group discussion, work experience, community projects, and student special interests. The staff included a director, secretary, three full-time teachers and two teaching interns, for a student body of fifty students.

The three full-time teachers were on a performance contract with the school district. They were promised a bonus at the end of the year if the project's nine objectives were satisfactorily completed. The final evaluation of the program, in 1971, conducted by a team of college professors, concluded that I-Team had met all nine objectives and the school board paid the bonus.

I-Team exemplified the possibility that performance contracting can break away from heavy reliance on test scores. Here are the nine objectives and their "measurement" or observation:

1) A model was to be developed for interdisciplinary student-centered experiences for educationally handicapped secondary students.

   Evaluators judged this successful because such a document was prepared by the staff which reflected their work during the year.

2) Teacher-developed methods and materials would be created.

   Evaluators discussed this objective with teachers, observed materials that had been created for instruction, for testing and for record-keeping, and concluded the objective had been met.

3) Teaching materials would emphasize applications of conceptual knowledge rather than abstract fact.

   Here evaluators examined the materials themselves. They also analyzed teacher and student reports about the program.

4) An environment would be created for "successful" educational experiences which provide the opportunity for "increased achievement levels." The presumption was that if these students learned, the new environment at I-Team was responsible.

   Evaluators looked at ratio of successes to failures. There were virtually no failures. Also, standardized achievement tests were administered. Gains averaged 2.0 years in reading and 3.3 years in math.

5) The environment would provide educational experiences leading to successful "adjustments to the school situation."

   Teacher reports, student reports, reduction of vandalism to zero, increased attendance, and pretest/posttest evidence from a Semantic Differential Test all demonstrated success.

6) The environment would produce attitudinal changes toward school and education.

   This was evaluated from student and teacher reports.

7) Students would become more involved in development of the instructional situations in which they learn.

   Students and teacher reports affirmed this and recommended still greater student involvement in future years.

8) Students would develop "social awareness."

   Evidence was sought in student reports, in special community projects completed, in changes of student courtesy, and respect toward each other. Evaluators were least satisfied with fulfillment of this objective.

9) Students would have opportunities to become involved in the "real world of work."

   Virtually every student held at least one job, with student reports indicating satisfaction and success.

In the opinion of the evaluation team, the bonus feature of the program was an effective incentive:

The Cherry Creek School District has justified the premise that performance contracting does have a place. The place is within the school district, by the district standards and objectives, and by the district personnel. . . .

This feature which provides incentive pay to *teachers within the district* (not to commercial educational entrepreneurs) would seem to have merit. Each of the involved staff members noted some concern relative to his effectiveness in achieving his bonus. No ill effects have been noted so far. This recommendation is for increasing the number of staff members who might receive such a bonus. . . . (8)

In 1971-1972, several other programs in Cherry Creek arranged similar incentive plans for teachers or administrators of special programs. (9)

Notes

(1) G. Gallup, "The Third Annual Survey of the Public's Attitudes Toward the Public Schools, 1971," *Phi Delta Kappan,* 53 (September 1971): 33-48; "The Things That School Leaders Like Best—and Least," *American School Board Journal,* 159 (July 1971): 13-15; "Teacher Opinion Poll: Accountability, Vouchers and Performance Contracting," *Today's Education,* 60 (December 1971): 13.

(2) Ibid.

(3) Stated by Roald Campbell, in discussion at the National Conference on Performance Contracting, Elkridge, Maryland, December 10, 1971.

(4) Grand Rapids Education Association, *GREA Times,* "Editorial," Sept./Oct., 1971.

(5) D. P. Barnard; H. W. Crawford; R. M. Jones; and J. R. Turner, "Project Directors' Perception of 'Incentives Only' Project," submitted to the Office of Economic Opportunity, January, 1972.

(6) C. Stalford, speaking to National School Boards Association conference on performance contracting, Chicago, Illinois, February 5, 1971.

(7) In addition to these contracts, Duval County was an OEO site, with Learning Foundations, Inc. Dallas was an OEO site with Quality Educational Development. Dallas also held a reading and mathematics contract with New Century.

(8) D. A. Brown, and D. Carline, *The I-Team Project: A Final Report,* submitted to Cherry Creek Public Schools, Cherry Creek, Colorado, June, 1971, pp. 44-45. Mimeographed.

(9) See J. A. Mecklenburger and J. A. Wilson, "Performance Contracting in Cherry Creek?!", *Phi Delta Kappan,* 53 (September 1971): 51-54.

X

Conclusion

As a modest tool for introducing change in school districts, many futures are open to performance contracting. The drama inherent in signing a performance contract, with its focus on results, makes it easier to change educational processes.

While some contracts may continue in the Texarkana mold, performance contracting is likely to evolve in other directions. It may acquire new names, particularly as teachers enter into such contracts. Under whatever terminology, the performance contract concept can be adapted in practice to any school subject and with any student population.

To do performance contracting well, and to avoid some of the pitfalls of the early contracts described in this study, the critical element is evaluation. Both change and evaluation are fraught with political dangers in education. "Never have so few scared so many with so little!" Charles Blaschke often remarks, paraphrasing Winston Churchill. Performance contracting is not a practice for the timid, for it is capable of causing harsh, irrational, political and legal retaliation, as Texarkana and Banneker illustrate. For these reasons, too, it is not a panacea; yet, some projects have resulted in rapid and significant innovation, so that performance contracting can be worth the dangers.

If, as a political-historical event, from 1969-1971, performance contracting was most akin to drama, the reader of this book should now understand this drama from many perspectives: he knows the plot, the characters, and the actors; he has visited several production companies and seen excerpts from several performances; he has explored the playwright's intentions, found some sources of his ideas, and read some of the reviews; and he knows how the play has been adapted and might be adapted.

Some participants in the play have claimed it is "revolutionary." There are many reasons to deny that claim. The ideas are not new. Measured in dollars or number of participants, measured by growth or by professional acceptance, measured by radical new techniques or outstanding results, two years of performance contracts have done less than perform major surgery on public education.

But if, as Hamlet thought, revolutions are in the mind, and one can connive with a mere play to "catch the conscience of the king," then performance contracts have acted in a revolutionary fashion. They offer a mirror into which public education has peered with chagrin. In this play, contractors did what public schools are reluctant to do: made promises about student learning they would be expected to fulfill. Theirs was a pragmatic, impatient, systematic approach to schooling; it was bolder, riskier, and more political than most educators would have found comfortable.

If one believes that schools should be effective in their tasks, then American education is better off for the example of performance contracting—however imperfectly realized in practice, and whether or not it continues—than had it not occurred at all. How much has been learned in the mirror, time will tell.

The Charles A. Jones Publishing Company

International Series in Education